THE TENNESSEE CruiseGuide®

by Fred Myers

A DEDICATION

I met Dyess Hartley by chance on the Tennessee River one May evening in 1989. He and his family were headed toward the Great Lakes aboard his cruiser.

As we visited, he erased the doubts I expressed about publishing a cruising guide for the Tennessee, urged me to continue with the project, and shared his opinions as to what the guide should be. I learned that Dyess was a successful businessman as well as a boater. Many years before, he had started a small printing plant in Jacksonville, Florida, and had built it into one of the finest in the southeastern U.S.

Dyess offered his help in the printing of the book and I accepted. He became my mentor as he guided this book as if it were his own through the first edition printings.

Although Dyess died shortly afterward, his influence lives on. Hartley Press, still a family business, continues to print my books. And each time I cruise the Tennessee I sense his presence.

To his memory I dedicate this Third Edition.

Fred Myers
Author and Publisher

First Edition	1990
Second Printing	1991
Second Edition	1995
Third Edition	1998

Copyright © 1998 by Fred Myers.
ISBN 0-9632005-6-9

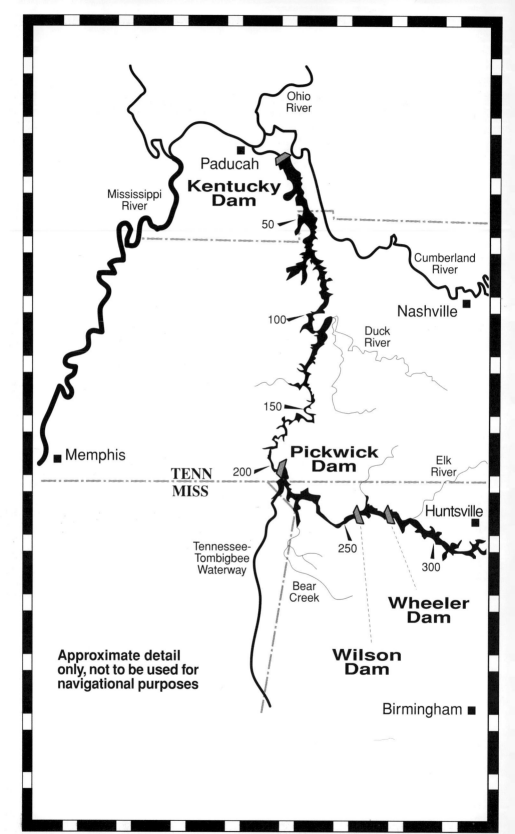

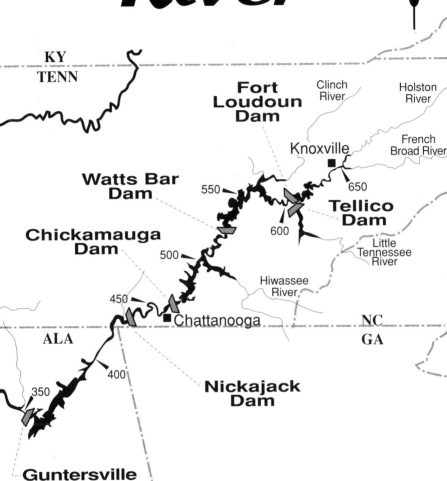

The Tennessee River

N

KY
TENN

Fort
Loudoun
Dam

Clinch
River

Holston
River

Knoxville

French
Broad River

Watts Bar
Dam

550

650

Tellico
Dam

Chickamauga
Dam

600

Little
Tennessee
River

500

450

Hiwassee
River

Chattanooga

NC

GA

ALA

400

Nickajack
Dam

350

Guntersville
Dam

Atlanta

THE TENNESSEE RIVER
CruiseGuide®

Author & Publisher:	**Fred Myers**
Designer:	**Wray Graphics** Florence, Alabama
Printer:	**The Hartley Press, Inc.** Jacksonville, Florida

About The Author

During his 41 years as a professional writer and photographer, Fred Myers has traveled throughout all 50 states, in several foreign countries, and around the world. Many of his quieter times between assignments, however, have been spent on boats. As a resident of northern Alabama for 36 years, he has extensive knowledge of the region's waterways and the surrounding country-side. During the last nine years, he has logged more than 17,000 miles on the Tennessee River, the Cumberland River, and the Tennessee-Tombigbee Waterway. The other books by Fred are *The Cumberland River CruiseGuide* and *The Tenn-Tom Nitty-Gritty CruiseGuide*.

Copies of this book are available by mail for $22.00 per copy, postpaid. Direct all orders and inquiries to *The Tennessee River CruiseGuide*, 803 Hermitage Drive, Suite 112, Florence, Alabama 35630 or call 256-766-4802. E-mail address: writerfred@AOL.com

FRONT COVER: On a quiet August morning near Daymark 432.4, the author's trawler "Liberty Belle" heads upstream toward the Grand Canyon of the Tennessee.

Contents

REFERENCE SECTION

CRUISE SECTION

No one could remember a spring lasting so long and a summer being so late.

For the more than two weeks we had been on the upper Tennessee, there had been rain or wind or cold. Sometimes, all three combined to give us plenty of cause for, as they say in these parts, "hunkerin down."

Still, we had managed to nudge the bow of our "Liberty Belle" into all the familiar marinas and coves. We even found some new water to cruise while on the upper reaches of Tellico Lake.

Now on the return and weary of leaden skies, we pulled into Goose Pond Marina on Guntersville Lake where we decided to spend the night and sit at the dock for a day. The next morning, as if on cue, we were greeted with a clear sky and a light warm wind.

We already knew that aside from being able to relax a bit, we also would be able to welcome a special group of boaters coming upriver that was spending the night at Goose Pond. The group consisted of more than 100 people from throughout the U.S. who had begun an organized trip up the Tennessee a few days earlier. What made them special is that they were making the 600 mile trip aboard their personal water craft.

By mid afternoon, they had begun to arrive, refuel and tie up. Soon, the dock was lined with the splashes of color of their craft and filled with tired people shaking out the kinks, checking out their boats, and enjoying the sun and warmth as much as we were.

As we mingled and visited with them, we discovered that this was the first time most of them had experienced the Tennessee. They talked excitedly about what they had seen and despite their tiredness, were anxious to get back on the water again the next morning.

Their enthusiasm wasn't surprising. No matter where boaters come from or how many years they have cruised, they are deeply impressed by the Tennessee. Again and again, they confirm that it offers some of the finest cruising in America.

To briefly share that experience with you is appropriate for introducing you to this Third Edition.

All information has been updated and bits and pieces have been added. For example, there is now mile by mile coverage of the Hiawassee, a major tributary of the Tennessee. But remaining are the main features that have made this cruising guide so popular among thousands of boaters.

I sincerely hope this book serves you well and that your journey on the Tennessee is safe, enjoyable and memorable.

Fred Myers

Fred Myers
Author and Publisher

WARNING! This book is not for navigational purposes nor is it intended to be used as a substitute for government navigation charts and other official documents. The author and publisher disclaims any liability for loss or damage to property or persons which may occur as a result of using or interpreting any information contained in this book.

This book is easy to use. It's small and lightweight for use at the helm. The spiral binding allows you to quickly find and keep the proper page in front of you. Space on each page of the Cruise Section plus other blank spaces allows you to enter your own notes.

Far more detail could have been included. But that would have defeated the goal of offering a concise, yet reasonably complete summary of what you want to know about cruising the Tennessee River.

Again, don't consider this book as a substitute for official publications and charts. In fact, to get the most from the CruiseGuide, you should use it as a supplement to the official charts.

The first section is the Reference Section. Read it carefully so you know how you can quickly access specific information.

The much larger Cruise Section describes the river beginning at Mile 0.0 at Paducah, Kentucky, and ending at Mile 652.0 near Knoxville, Tennessee, where the Tennessee River begins.

Indicated along the margin of each page are "DAYMARK" or "MILE." DAYMARK refers to a specific navigation aid on the river shown on the official charts. MILE indicates an estimated location as it relates to navigational aids and other physical objects.

The other margin designations, MARINA, FUEL, REPAIR FACILITY, LODGING, RESTAURANT, FOOD, RESORT, DOCKAGE, and ANCHORAGE quickly identify the locations of these services.

Directions for finding each marina and anchorage are related to natural features as much as possible. This will prove helpful whether you are using the CruiseGuide to go upstream or downstream.

Facilities aren't judged or rated because personal tastes and conditions under which you might use these facilities are far too variable.

Although descriptions of marina services have been verified, any service not listed probably isn't available. But marina ownership and services may change. So if a particular service is important to you, call ahead.

Not all restaurants at a given location are listed. But those that are can be easily reached and are often recommended to transient boaters.

Some of the listed anchorages are already indicated on official charts as First Class or Second Class harbors. Others were recommended by local boaters and marina operators. Still others are ones the author believes worthy of your attention. Unless otherwise noted, water depths refer to the center or near center of each embayment.

Finally, there is much to see and do along and near the Tennessee. Contact the information sources listed at the back of the CruiseGuide and tell them of your special interests.

The River Called The Tennessee

The Tennessee, one of the Nation's great rivers, drains an area of about 40,000 square miles. It's the largest tributary of the Ohio River and in terms of streamflow is the seventh largest in the United States.

It begins just east of Knoxville, Tennessee, with the joining of the Holston River and the French Broad River. Headwaters for the Holston are in the rolling hills of southwest Virginia. The French Broad begins east of the Great Smoky Mountains.

From Knoxville, the Tennessee flows southwest through east Tennessee, into northeast Alabama before turning westward across Alabama's northern tier of counties to the northeastern tip of Mississippi.

At that point, the river turns north, flows through western Tennessee and Kentucky, and joins the Ohio River at Paducah, Kentucky.

Clearly, the Tennessee doesn't flow logically. Water from east of the Smoky Mountains cuts through those mountains to join the Tennessee instead of flowing eastward to the Atlantic. The main river cuts through the Cumberland Plateau instead of going around it and turns northward for 200 miles toward the Ohio River instead of continuing westward and joining the much closer Mississippi River.

First visited by the Spanish explorer DeSoto in 1540, the Tennessee became a vital route for other explorers and for settlers. But for early boaters, traveling the Tennessee was far from easy. There were whirlpools, sand bars, and snags. Winter and spring rains often caused the river to become a raging torrent.

Also, freight boats were limited to the upper and lower ends of the river. Rapids at Muscle Shoals, Alabama, prevented boats from traveling the entire length. In the 15 miles between the present Wheeler Dam and Wilson Dam, the river dropped nearly 100 feet.

Boats arriving at Muscle Shoals had to be unloaded, pulled by horses past the rapids, then reloaded. It was time consuming and back breaking work. Not until 1890 were the rapids bypassed by a canal containing several locks.

In 1913, Hales Bar Dam was completed about 35 miles downstream from Chattanooga. It was the first attempt to use the river's water power to generate electricity. And in 1918, the Department of the Army decided to build a dam at Muscle Shoals to generate power for a munitions plant and to create deep water for navigation on that part of the river.

Then in 1933, the Tennessee Valley Authority (TVA) was created as part of President Roosevelt's New Deal. The TVA promised electric power and a program of resource development to the people of the Valley, most of whom were economically destitute.

The main thrust of that effort was the building of dams. There are nine of them on the river. All have navigation locks. First is Kentucky Dam just upstream from where the Tennessee joins the Ohio River at Paducah, followed by Pickwick Dam, Wilson Dam which has the world's third highest single lift lock, Wheeler Dam, Guntersville Dam, Nickajack Dam, Chickamauga Dam near Chattanooga, Watts Bar Dam, and Fort Loudoun Dam which is a few miles downstream from Knoxville.

With these dams plus many others on the Tennessee's tributaries, TVA is able to prevent disastrous floods, generate tremendous amounts of hydroelectric power, and provide a deep and dependable navigation channel for the entire 652-mile length of the river.

Although creating recreational opportunities wasn't one of TVA's most important goals, local boaters have long appreciated the Tennessee. Now, its fame is spreading as increasing numbers of boaters are discovering that the Tennessee offers some of the Nation's finest freshwater cruising.

The Tennessee has more than a thousand square miles of water surface and about 11,000 miles of shoreline. The shoreline of Kentucky Lake alone is longer than that of the entire west coast of the United States.

Because the Tennessee takes an unusual course through both mountains and flatlands, its banks are never monotonous. In places, they are so low you can see the fields beyond. But in others, cliffs tower hundreds of feet above the river.

To cruise the Tennessee is also to see a slice of America. There are small farms, large cities, and remnants of Indian and pioneer cultures mixed with striking evidence of today's technology.

Whether you travel all or only part of it, there's a good chance the Tennessee will provide you with many pleasant memories.

Important Notes About Navigating

Those who have traveled on the Tennessee, especially commercial towboat pilots, consider the river one of the most well marked and easiest to navigate of all the inland waterways.

Remarkable in itself is the fact that there is a guaranteed 9-foot navigation channel for all but the last three miles of its 652-mile length.

Many well placed and well maintained navigational aids plus 24-hour operation of all but Fort Loudoun lock make travel possible both day and night. Also, more than 200 miles of the river's tributaries are marked with buoys and other navigational aids.

Just remember the direction in which you are going. If you are a Midwestern boater, you are accustomed to going downstream on such rivers as the Ohio and Mississippi. When you enter the Tennessee at Paducah, your brain insists you are still going "down." That's true in terms of heading south but the fact is, you're going upstream. That can be very confusing.

One marina manager says he knows a boater in Cincinnati who had this problem. After almost running aground as a result of cruising on the wrong side of the red buoys, the Ohio boater mounted a short piece of wood at the helm with a red knob on one end and a green knob on the other. When he enters the Tennessee, he switches the knobs as a constant reminder of "red right returning."

Perhaps the most important aspect of navigating the Tennessee is knowing the pool level of each of the nine lakes. Lake levels don't vary enough during summer to cause concern among boaters except during extremely dry or wet years. During late winter and spring, heavy rains can cause the river to rise to flood stage.

You should know, however, that during the summer, TVA begins to lower water levels as part of its overall water management plan for the river.

The drawdown begins on Kentucky Lake in early July and is completed on the upper reaches of the river by early December. The maximum drawdown is about five feet upriver as far as Chattanooga and about seven feet upriver from Chattanooga to Knoxville.

Water level gages are at each dam and at other locations along the river. By reading the gages as you pass them you can add or subtract any deviation of the reading from what the gage would read at normal pool level and add or subtract that figure from the normal pool level given for each lake to determine actual pool level.

Lake levels are broadcast at certain times of the day by the local NOAA weather stations which you can access on VHF channels WX 1, 2, or 3. The Coast Guard, Ohio Valley Group, gives lake levels in its announcements to navigational interests. It alerts boaters on channel 16 then provides the information a few seconds later on channel 22.

Also, you can call TVA's Lake Information Line at 1-800-238-2264. When the electronic voice answers, press 1 for observed lake elevations or press 2 for predicted lake elevations. Then press the two-number code for the lake in which you are interested. They are: Kentucky, 33; Pickwick, 32; Wilson, 31; Wheeler, 30; Guntersville, 29; Nickajack, 28; Chickamauga, 27; Watts Bar, 18; and Fort Loudoun, 08. Press the * key to return to the main menu. To exit the system, press 9 then hang up.

Once you know the pool level, you can easily determine approximate water depth. The Corps of Engineers charts show depths at normal pool level for different parts of the river bottom. Comparing those figures with actual pool level can help you choose a safe route as an alternative to the designated navigation channel.

Here's an example:

Suppose you are cruising upstream on Wheeler Lake and are nearing Decatur, Alabama. You decide at Mile 301.0 to leave the navigation channel and take a closer look at the river's bank at starboard.

The official navigation chart shows that the river bottom where you wish to leave the channel has an elevation of 538 feet above sea level. It also shows that just beyond, the contour of the river bottom increases to an elevation of 550 feet.

Now assume that you have seen from the charts that the elevation of Wheeler Lake at normal pool is 556 feet.

This means that as you leave the navigation channel, you can expect the water to be 556 minus 538 or 18 feet deep. It also means that very soon you will encounter water that's only six feet deep or 556 minus 550.

But what if there is a drought and the elevation of Wheeler Lake is only 551 feet instead of the normal pool of 556 feet? That means you have five feet less water under your boat.

Using the same example, you would have a water depth of 13 feet as you leave the navigation channel which would quickly decrease to one foot.

You can determine the pool level on any segment of the river by looking at the gages. In this case, the last gage you could have read would have been the one at Wheeler Dam. At normal pool, that gage reads 20. But in our "dry year" example above, the gage would read only 15.

All gage locations are given below. Some gages, however, may be difficult to read or have yet to be replaced after being damaged or missing as the result of high water.

Remember that the charts, as good as they are, can't be made completely accurate, that river conditions keep changing, and that indicated elevations of the river bottom don't consider underwater obstructions such as stumps. Good sense, slow speed, and paying attention to your depthfinder, however, will go a long way in keeping you out of trouble.

The following information, taken from official charts, is included here for your convenience.

LAKE:	NORMAL POOL ELEVATION (Feet above sea level):	LAKE:	NORMAL POOL ELEVATION (Feet above sea level):
Kentucky	359.0	Nickajack	634.0
Pickwick	414.0	Chickamauga	682.5
Wilson	507.5	Watts Bar	741.0
Wheeler	556.0	Ft. Loudoun	813.0
Guntersville	595.0		

GAGE LOCATION:	GAGE READS:

Paducah to Kentucky Dam

Mile 0	15.7 at normal pool
Mile 13.9	Elevation Direct
Kentucky Dam (lower lock wall)	12.7 at normal pool

Kentucky Lake

Kentucky Dam (upper lock wall)	24.0 at normal pool
Mile 41.7 (bridge)	Elevation direct
Mile 66.3 (bridge)	Elevation direct
Mile 78.2 (bridge)	Elevation direct
Mile 100.5 (bridge)	Elevation direct
Mile 134.9 (bridge)	Elevation direct
Mile 157.4	Elevation direct
Mile 169.2	Elevation direct
Mile 189.9 (bridge)	Elevation direct
Mile 192.1	Elevation direct
Mile 193.4	Elevation direct
Mile 195.2	Elevation direct
Mile 200.9	Elevation direct
Pickwick Dam (lower aux. lock wall)	16.8 at normal pool

Pickwick Lake

Pickwick Dam (upper aux. lock wall)	16.0 at normal pool
Mile 245.6	Elevation direct
Mile 256.4 (bridge)	Elevation direct
Wilson Dam (lower main lock wall)	19.0 at normal pool

Wilson Lake

Wilson Dam (upper main lock wall)	16.0 at normal pool
Wheeler Dam (lower main lock wall)	16.0 at normal pool

Wheeler Lake

Wheeler Dam (upper main lock wall)	20.0 at normal pool
Mile 305.0 (bridge)	Elevation direct
Mile 333.3 (bridge)	Elevation direct
Guntersville Dam (lower lock wall)	18.7 at normal pool

Guntersville Lake

Guntersville Dam (upper lock wall)	17.0 at normal pool
Mile 358.0 (bridge)	Elevation direct
Mile 385.8 (bridge)	Elevation direct
Mile 407.8	Elevation direct
Mile 414.4 (bridge)	Elevation direct
Nickajack Dam (lower lock wall)	15.0 at normal pool

Nickajack Lake

Nickajack Dam (upper lock wall)	15.5 at normal pool
Mile 431.1	Elevation direct
Mile 445.9	Elevation direct
Mile 464.1 (bridge)	Elevation direct
Mile 468.0	Elevation direct
Chickamauga Dam (lower lock wall)	15.8 at normal pool

Chickamauga Lake

Chickamauga Dam (upper lock wall)	19.5 at normal pool
Mile 476.0	Elevation direct
Mile 497.2	Elevation direct
Mile 499.2	Elevation direct
Mile 499.4 (bridge)	Elevation direct
Mile 503.7	Elevation direct
Mile 518.0	Elevation direct
Mile 523.2	Elevation direct
Watts Bar Dam (lower lock wall)	19.3 at normal pool

Watts Bar Lake

Watts Bar Dam (upper lock wall)	20.0 at normal pool
Mile 542.0	Elevation direct
Mile 556.5	Elevation direct
Mile 568.1 (bridge)	Elevation direct
Mile 575.9	Elevation direct
Mile 591.6 (bridge)	Elevation direct
Fort Loudoun Dam (lower lock wall)	17.8 at normal pool

Ft. Loudoun Lake

Fort Loudoun Dam (upper lock wall)	35.0 at normal pool
Mile 612.8	Elevation direct
Mile 619.1	Elevation direct
Mile 625.0	Elevation direct
Mile 639.0	Elevation direct
Mile 643.0	Elevation direct
Mile 647.4 (bridge)	Elevation direct
Mile 648.4 (bridge)	Elevation direct

Current on the Tennessee is affected by two variables, the amount of water being released through the hydroelectric generating plants and dams and where you are on the river.

Under normal conditions, TVA regulates the system to maintain the navigation channel while generating the most hydroelectric power possible with the amount of water available. In an extremely dry year, the flow is greatly restricted. When the river is at flood stage, as much water as possible is routed through the turbines and spillways consistent with the need to control flooding.

The second factor is the width of the river. The slowest current is just above each dam. The fastest is in the narrow part of the river just below each dam.

Also, there are three other locations where current tends to be greatest. They are: Below Kentucky Dam from about Mile 15.0 to Mile 19.0, below Pickwick Dam from about Mile 203.0 to Mile 206.0, and above Nickajack Dam from about Mile 443.0 to Mile 454.0.

Measurements made by TVA show that during a normal summer, current at these three locations and for about the first five miles below each dam won't exceed two miles per hour. More than likely, it will be a bit less than that. At all other locations, the current will be one mile per hour or less.

When the river is at flood stage, current at the three locations given above and for about the first five miles below each dam won't exceed six to seven miles per hour.

In short, current normally isn't a major concern. But if the river is near flood stage and your boat is limited in terms of forward speed, you would be wise to wait until streamflow is reduced.

Two bridges control vertical clearance on the Tennessee's navigation channel. One is the highway bridge across Pickwick Dam at Mile 206.7 with a vertical clearance of 52.0 feet at normal pool. The other is the railroad bridge at Mile 647.3, with a vertical clearance of 50.0 feet at normal pool. All other bridges have clearances of at least 56 feet at normal pool.

Three railway lift bridges cross the Tennessee, one at Mile 100.5, another at Mile 304.4, and another at Mile 414.1. Vertical clearances in the closed position and at normal pool are 24.6 feet, 9.8 feet, and 34.2 feet, respectively.

There are no longer any highway lift bridges on the Tennessee. The last one, at Decatur, Alabama, was replaced in 1997 by a stationary bridge.

All powerline crossings are constructed to be well above the minimum safe height for any sailboat mast short enough to pass under any of the bridges crossing the Tennessee.

This applies, however, only to crossings on the main river. Some powerlines crossing embayments and tributaries of the Tennessee are below those minimums and must be avoided by boats with high masts. Also, some of those crossings may not be on official charts.

If you need more specific information about river flow and lake elevations, call TVA at its main switchboard at 423-632-8000. For information on bridge clearances call TVA at 423-632-7157 or the Corps of Engineers at 615-736-5607.

How To Be Safe, Be Smart, And Stay Healthy

Here are some important precautions and suggestions to remember as you cruise the Tennessee River:

1. Areas just above and below all dams on the river are danger zones. They are indicated on official charts and are marked by warning signs and buoys. Because these dams produce electricity, there can be swirling water and strong underwater currents at powerhouse intakes. There also can be sudden discharges from automatically operated sluice and trash gates and from turbines. There are no sound or visual warnings to indicate when and to what degree these operations are about to occur. Except in the navigation channel, shallow water, rocks, and fast current are common hazards below the dams.

2. The river is popular with fishermen. Trot lines are common, particularly in shallower water. These lines have hooks at intervals and are supported by floats, usually plastic bottles. Stay clear of these floats to avoid getting the lines entangled in propellers. Also, if you should happen to hook a trot line with your anchor, try to remove the lines from the anchor after you retrieve it. Cut them only if necessary.

3. When cruising close to shore, watch for fishing boats leaving embayments at high speed.

4. Debris such as tree limbs, logs, and other trash is most common during the high rainfall months of February through April. Although relatively little debris floats in the river during the prime cruising months of May through November, watch for it at all times.

5. Watching your wake is important on the Tennessee. Most areas near marinas and narrow channels leading to them will be marked with no-wake signs or buoys. Obey them. Some marinas will sternly remind you on channel 16 to slow down if you fail to do so on your own. Slow down when approaching other boats, especially on narrow sections of the river and in narrower embayments where your wake could swamp other boats, damage docks, aggravate the erosion of the river's banks, and intrude on the enjoyment of others.

6. Steer clear of river tows. Cruising in front of one is exceedingly dangerous because the tow captain may not be able to see you or stop in time if you lose power or need to stop for any reason. Respect the wakes created by tows. The powerful engines and big propellers create a rolling turbulence that could cause you to lose control of your boat.

7. The wide expanses of open water can be deceiving. Be cautious when you leave a marked channel. Slow down, monitor your depthfinder, and look at the charts often to check your position. If you're interested in cruising a particular part of the river, ask local boaters and marina operators first about water depths and possible underwater hazards not indicated on charts.

8. Marine police representing each of their respective states patrol the river, especially in areas of heavy boat traffic. They have the same enforcement powers as their state police counterparts. At TVA facilities, uniformed public safety officers enforce the law. Keep in mind that offenses committed on TVA property come under Federal rather than State jurisdiction.

9. Discharging firearms over open water from a moving boat can get you into big trouble. Also, law enforcement agencies along the Tennessee are alert to the possible transporting, sale, and use of illegal drugs.

10. Operating a boat while under the influence of alcohol or any other drug is unlawful. The maximum legal limit for blood alcohol content is 0.10 percent or less and even a first offense penalty involves a heavy fine and jail sentence. Also, any person operating a boat on public waters implies willingness to undergo drug or alcohol testing. Refusal to submit to testing will result in a six month suspension of the privilege to operate any vessel subject to registration.

11. In case of emergency, make your situation known on channel 16. The Coast Guard, marine operator services, marinas, lockmasters, and other boaters monitor that channel and will try to help. It's probably

safe to say that no part of the river is so isolated that your call won't be heard. Remember, however, that having the proper safety equipment on board, having enough fuel, and properly maintaining your boat to reduce the chances of you needing help is a responsibility you should be willing to accept. Also, no boat is too small to carry a flare pistol and a first aid kit.

12. Many powerlines cross the Tennessee River and its tributaries. Sailboat masts shouldn't come within 15 feet of them. Or as one veteran sailor said, "If it does, you would do well to slather yourself in barbeque sauce right then and there." Vertical clearances given on the official charts are measured from the low points of sag. Also, there may be powerlines crossing minor tributaries not shown on official charts. For more information, call TVA at 423-632-7157.

13. The navigation locks and narrow stretches of the Tennessee River can be particularly confining and made more challenging by wind and current. Power boaters should understand that according to the Rules of the Road, they are to give sailboats under sail the right of way in all situations. Even sailboats under power have limited maneuverability. In more open water, sailboats should be given wide berth and low wake in meeting and crossing situations. At the same time, sailboaters should be aware of the limits of their boats so they won't be endangered by such things as current, lack of maneuvering space, or the inability to get out of the way of river tows.

14. Fog is always a hazard to boaters but even more so on rivers where sounds and their direction are distorted. When in doubt, stay put and wait it out.

15. If you decide to pull into a cove and take a swim, remember that much of the land under water on the Tennessee River is flooded farmland. Just out of sight may be such nasties as stumps or fence posts with barbed wire. Swim around your boat and check out the water before you jump or dive in.

16. It's against Federal law to dump anything in a river or stream under Federal control. More important, you should be willing to do your part in helping keep the Nation's waterways clean and beautiful. Use pump out stations and take advantages of sanitary facilities on shore whenever possible. Keep all trash and garbage on board until you can properly dispose of it. The Mote Marine Laboratory, Sarasota, Florida, has compiled figures showing how much time is needed for items often dumped in our waterways to degrade. These examples may surprise you:

Paper towel	4 weeks
Cardboard box	2 months
Tin can	50 years
Styrofoam cup	50 years
Aluminum can	200 years
Disposable diaper	450 years
Plastic bottle	450 years
Monofilament fishing line	600 years

What You Should Know About Locking Through

Important! A lock can be closed for several days or weeks for repair. As part of your trip planning, call the Corps of Engineers in Nashville, Tennessee, at 615-736-5607 to find out if any locks are scheduled to be closed.

All locks on the Tennessee River operate 24 hours a day except the lock at Fort Loudoun Dam which operates from 6AM until 10PM. All monitor VHF channel 16.

Although lockmasters on the Tennessee are known for their friendliness, they do enforce the rules. Cooperating with them will result in faster and more troublefree lockages.

The Secretary of the Army has established a priority for passing boats through locks. U.S. Government vessels are at the top of the list followed by commercial passenger vessels, commercial tows or vessels, and pleasure boats, in that order. Normally, locking through will take less than an hour. But you might be delayed either by other boats with a higher priority being locked through or by a large number of boats trying to lock through at the same time. Be patient!

Stay in the navigation channel when you approach a lock. You can signal the lockmaster by giving one long blast and one short blast with your horn, by pulling the signal cord in the ladder recess near the end of the approach wall, or by calling on channel 16 which is monitored by every lockmaster.

Obey the traffic signals. Flashing red means the lock can't be made ready immediately; stand clear and don't attempt to enter the lock. Flashing amber means the lock is being made ready; you may approach the lock guide wall but don't enter the lock. Flashing green means the lock is ready; you can enter the lock. Also, the lockmaster will signal you to enter with a horn blast.

Remember that the lockmaster has full authority over the movement of boats in and near the lock. If you willfully disobey orders, you could be cited or even jailed for violating Federal regulations. That doesn't happen often. But when it does, liquor is most often the cause.

Be prepared. Make sure fenders are in place to prevent your boat from hitting the lock wall. The person tending the lines must wear a lifejacket. Keep everybody well inside your boat while locking through. For example, no one should be sitting on the bow or swim platform.

Enter a lock at idle speed. If you don't, your wake will cause rough water inside the lock which will make it difficult not only for other boaters but also for you.

Once inside, you will be tying your boat to a floating mooring post recessed in the lock wall. There's one way to tie up a boat in a lock that works perfectly almost every time. Here's how you do it:

Place two or three fenders so your boat won't touch the wall even if it turns at a slight angle. That means a fender a short distance from the bow, another about a third of the way from the bow, and the last one a short distance from the stern. Then tie a line to a midship cleat. Maneuver your boat until it's close to the wall and the floating mooring post is even with the cleat. Then make two counterclockwise turns around the post with your line before tying it off to the cleat.

Your boat is now free to pivot. As it does, the fenders will prevent it from touching the wall. By taking two turns around the post instead of just one, you will prevent excessive forward or backward movement of your boat. Your line will stay cleaner because by being wrapped counterclockwise around the post, it will come off the front of the post and hardly ever touch the dirty lock walls.

If you have a smaller boat with no center cleat or if your boat has only a narrow ledge along the side, tie a line to the bow cleat, run it the length of your boat, and tie it temporarily to the stern cleat. Do this before you enter the lock. When you're ready to tie up to the mooring post, untie the line from the stern cleat, take the two counterclockwise turns around the post, then tie off the line to the cleat. You can do this from the cockpit.

Don't panic and don't get in a hurry if you have a problem getting your boat properly positioned and tied up. Take your time and do it right.

You may be tempted to push against the grimy lock walls with your hands. Don't do it, even if you are wearing gloves. It's much safer and cleaner to use a boat hook.

Expect your boat to move around more when you're locking upstream. That's because as the lock fills, water flows up, under, and past your boat. Generally, there is greater turbulence toward the center of the lock. When you're locking downstream, that won't happen because water will be draining from the lock.

There are no regulations requiring your engines and generators to be shut off during lockage. But because locks, especially the smaller and deeper ones, are relatively closed spaces, you may want to turn your engines off to help prevent a buildup of exhaust fumes. Also, it's best to avoid all open flames.

Keep your boat tied until the lockmaster gives the horn signal. Boats nearest the exit should leave first. Use idle speed as you follow the boats in front of you and until you are well clear of the lock.

Locks on the Tennessee attract many tourists and onlookers, especially on weekends. If you have an audience when you lock through, take time from your boating duties to enjoy it!

Here's a list of the locks on the Tennessee River. Refer to the Cruise Section for more information regarding approaches to these locks.

DAM	LOCK CHAMBER DIMENSIONS	NORMAL LIFT	TELEPHONE
Kentucky	600' X 110'	57'	502-362-4226
Pickwick Main	1000' X 110'	55'	901-925-2334
Pickwick Auxiliary	600' X 110'		
Wilson*	600' X 110'	93'	256-764-5223
Wheeler Main	600' X 110'	48'	256-247-3311
Wheeler Auxiliary	400' X 60'		
Guntersville Main	600' X 110'	39'	256-582-3263
Guntersville Auxiliary	360' X 60'		
Nickajack	600' X 110'	39'	423-942-3985
Chickamauga	360' X 60'	48'	423-622-8013
Watts Bar	360' X 60'	59'	423-334-3522
Fort Loudoun**	360' X 60'	72'	423-986-2762

*Auxiliary lock used only in emergency
**Operates only 6AM to 10PM, all others operate 24 hours

Many boaters prefer to anchor out rather than tie up at a marina dock. They may enjoy the quiet privacy, the sounds of nature, and relish the fact that the only cost is a little time and effort. For them, the hundreds of embayments and coves along the banks of the Tennessee offer many fine possibilities.

To prevent confusion and needless detail, only a few carefully selected anchorages are described. They are, however, among those most often suggested by other boaters and marinas, are reasonably easy to enter, and are strategically located.

You can anchor just about anywhere except in areas where it's specifically prohibited such as in navigation channels, near locks and dams, and over or near pipelines and other utility crossings.

But with that privilege comes responsibility. If you anchor near riverfront homes, watch your wake as well as your behavior which includes not creating excessive noise or dumping waste overboard.

Several anchorages described in the CruiseGuide are shown on the official charts as a First Class harbor or Second Class harbor. This is for the benefit of commercial shipping interests, not pleasure boaters. The upper limit of each of the harbors is usually marked on the bank with white crosses. Whenever and wherever possible, you should anchor beyond them so you will be well out of the way if a commercial tow enters the harbor. For the same reason, you shouldn't tie up to pilings in these harbors.

Rarely will the river bottom consist of anything other than mud. But here are two helpful hints. First, if you are using a Fortress anchor, the mud palms will help. But don't reset the angle of penetration for mud. That's for soft mud, not for the sticky kind found on the bottom of the Tennessee. Second, you may find that a plow (CQR) anchor is more effective where there are heavy infestations of hydrilla and water milfoil because it will more easily penetrate the vegetation.

In many locations, there is debris such as stumps and limbs on the river bottom. Trying to retrieve an anchor that's become lodged in debris can be aggravating and you may even lose the anchor. The answer is to always use a trip line.

You can quickly rig one by tying a piece of line to a fender or milk jug. The line should be a bit longer than the water depth in which you will be
anchoring. Tie the other end to the stock or fluke end of your anchor. If your anchor becomes wedged on the bottom and you can't pull it up, move

your boat so you can use the trip line to pull the anchor backward from the way it was set. Also, because the buoy indicates your swinging area, it can prevent others from dropping their anchor over your line.

All About The Weather

Because of its flattened "U" shaped course, the Tennessee River fits into an east-west rectangle about 250 miles long and 175 miles wide. So weather conditions don't change much from one end of the river to the other.

The last freezing temperatures in spring occur in early April and return in late October. Typical summer temperatures range from the high 60's to low 70's at night to the high 80's and low to mid 90's in daytime.

Western Kentucky and west Tennessee are far enough west and north to sometimes benefit from occasional cool fronts that move south from the Midwest during the summer. But seldom are they strong enough to push into northern Alabama and eastern Tennessee. As a result, there can be long periods of heat and humidity.

Average annual precipitation throughout the Valley region ranges from about 45 inches in the west to 55 inches in the east. Much of that is rain that falls during February, March, and April. This is reflected in how TVA regulates the Tennessee River. During the fall and winter months, water levels are lowered on both the main river and on 23 tributary lakes.

By preparing the system for storing runoff resulting from spring rains, flooding is prevented or greatly reduced. Also, the stored water can then be used for navigation and production of electric power later in the year.

It's during the fall drawdown that boaters begin to experience lower than normal pool levels. This is a gradual process that doesn't seriously interfere with fall boating.

The Tennessee Valley, however, has experienced extremes in recent years. In 1988, the Valley was in its third consecutive year of extreme drought. Water levels were the lowest in history. Although the navigation channel was kept open throughout the length of the river, many embayments became too shallow for boats.

But in 1989, rainfall returned to normal during the first few months of the year. Then in June, rainfall amounts throughout the region not only estab-lished a record for the month but in some locations came close to or exceeded the record for any month in recorded history.

As a result, spillways were opened as water levels surged upward. Also, debris which had been accumulating for several years along the banks began floating down the river. Boating was possible but it required great caution. Almost the same conditions were repeated in September when total rainfall was the second highest for any September in 100 years.

The point is, the Tennessee is great for cruising because it is one of the world's best and most carefully regulated rivers. But boaters must understand that some conditions can't be controlled.

Summer storms are common on the Tennessee River and although they usually don't last long, they often produce high winds and waves and dangerous lightning. These storms most often come from the west and southwest but there are exceptions.

For example, some boaters still remember the afternoon of July 4, 1982, when a particularly strong storm raked Lake Wilson with winds so strong that smaller boats were endangered. It came straight out of the north.

On a May evening in 1989, a marina on Pickwick Lake was hit by a sudden and brief storm so strong that large boats docked in transient slips heeled over by as much as 30 degrees. The storm came from the east which "never" happens.

The lesson is clear. Boaters on the Tennessee River should be aware of the potential for storms and be prepared to head for protection.

As you would expect, fog is most common in spring and fall when there's the greatest chance of sharp differences between air and water temperatures. Fog is particularly likely on the river in the vicinity of the Sequoyah nuclear power plant at Mile 484.0. This is because of the release of warm water into the river from the plant's cooling system.

Sailing is best during the spring and fall months. In fact, many sailors don't try to do much serious sailing during July and August because of summer heat and the lack of wind.

Autumn foliage in the Tennessee Valley is spectacular, particularly in the eastern end of the valley between Chattanooga and Knoxville where there is plenty of hardwood forest. Generally, peak color occurs during the last two weeks of October. But because autumn comes gradually to the South, there is often considerable color throughout most of the month and even well into November.

Radiotelephone:

Marine Telephone Company (Maritel) has relay towers that provide service on the Tennessee from Mile 0.0 at Paducah to about Mile 300.0 at Decatur, Alabama. The same service extends southward along the Tenn-Tom Waterway from its junction with the Tennessee to Demopolis, Alabama. For more information, call 1-800-955-9025.

To make contact with this service while on most of Kentucky Lake, call the marine operator on channel 85. Upstream to the limit of coverage, use channel 86. If you can't make contact, try using channel 16. Once you make contact, the marine operator will switch you to another channel to take your call.

There are no radiotelephone services upstream from about Mile 300.0 on Wheeler Lake.

Cellular Telephone:

There is good cellular phone coverage along most of the Tennessee. Poorest coverage is on the upper reaches of Kentucky Lake in the vicinity of Mile 95.0 and Mile 150.0. Coverage, however, often depends on antenna length and height, terrain, weather, and the type of equipment you are using.

VHF Marine Radio:

Assuming you have average VHF equipment, it's nearly impossible for you to be out of radio range of another boat, a lockmaster at one of the dams, or a marina.

Also, if you have an emergency and are unable to contact anyone else, you will nearly always be able to communicate with the Coast Guard, Group Ohio Valley. It has relay facilities along the entire length of the Tennessee and monitors channel 16.

Finally, remember that channel 16 is to be used only for calling. Once you establish contact, move to another channel to keep channel 16 open and available for other users. Channels 68 and 72 are most widely used for communicating between pleasure boats.

The Tennessee-Tombigbee Waterway and Cumberland River

The idea of connecting the Tombigbee River with the Tennessee River was first mentioned more than 250 years ago. In the years to follow, such a project was proposed several times. But in 1985, after many environmental and funding battles, the Tennessee-Tombigbee Waterway, or Tenn-Tom as it's most often called, finally became a reality.

It was a gigantic project. More excavating was required for it than for the Panama Canal and the cost was almost $2 billion. In fact, it was the largest and most costly project ever undertaken by the U.S. Army Corps of Engineers.

The Tombigbee River begins in a range of hills about 30 miles south of the Tennessee River. The waterway's canal section cuts through that divide. The narrow and twisting upper reaches of the Tombigbee were widened and straightened and 10 locks and dams were built.

With the Tenn-Tom, boaters now can go north on the Black Warrior-Tombigbee Waterway from Mobile, Alabama, on the Gulf Coast, to Demopolis, Alabama, enter the Tenn-Tom, then join the Tennessee at Mile 215.3 on Pickwick Lake.

An increasing number of pleasure boaters are discovering that using the Tenn-Tom between the Midwest and the Gulf Coast is a shorter, easier, and much safer route than traveling the Mississippi River.

Charts of the Tenn-Tom are available from the Corps of Engineers. Also, more information is available from the Tennessee-Tombigbee Waterway Development Authority, P.O. Drawer 671, Columbus, Mississippi 39703-0671, phone 601-328-3286.

The Cumberland River is another river that has a close kinship with the Tennessee. Not only do both rivers empty into the Ohio River only nine miles apart, but the rivers parallel each other for almost 100 miles. The land between them for much of that distance is the Land Between The Lakes National Recreation Area.

The Cumberland's navigation channel extends for 381 miles past Clarksville, Tennessee, through downtown Nashville, Tennessee, and skirts the Cumberland Plateau before ending at Celina, Tennessee.

Although the Cumberland is scenic and quiet for much of its length and easily reached from the Tennessee by a short canal, it remains undiscovered by many pleasure boaters.

Navigation charts for the Cumberland are available from the Corps of Engineers.

Distance and Trip Planning Chart

Location	Approximate River Mile		Fuel G-Gas D-Diesel
Paducah, Kentucky		0.0	
Kentucky Lock & Dam		22.4	
Kentucky Dam Marina		23.0	G, D
Anchorage (Sledd Creek)		23.0	
Lighthouse Landing Marina		24.1	G, D
Green Turtle Bay Marina		24.8	G, D
LBL Anchorages	25.4		
Pisgah Bay	30.1		
Smith Bay	32.5		
Duncan Bay	34.0		
Sugar Bay	35.7		
Moors Resort & Marina		29.1	G
Kenlake State Park Marina		41.9	G, D
Anchorage (Ledbetter Creek)		41.9	
Harbor Hill Marine		44.2	G, D
Anchorage (Clay Bay)		54.3	
Anchorage (Cypress Creek)		62.6	
Paris Landing State Park Marina		64.4	G, D
Anchorage (Bass Bay)		79.7	
Anchorage (Crooked Creek)		83.8	
Birdsong Resort & Marina		103.5	G, D
Cuba Landing Marina		115.5	G, D
Anchorage (Densons Island)		125.0	
Michael's Perryville Marina		135.0	G, D
Gumdale Marina		140.0	G, D
Anchorage (Kelleys Island)		143.0	
Anchorage (Double Islands)		148.5	
Anchorage (Beech Creek Island)		155.0	
Clifton City Marina		158.5	G

Anchorage (Indian Creek)	168.3	
Scotty's Saltillo Marina	171.8	G
Anchorage (Diamond Island)	195.3	
Pickwick Lock & Dam	206.7	
Pickwick Landing State Park Marina	207.6	G, D
Anchorage (Dry Creek)	209.6	
Pickwick's Tenn-Tom Marina	215.3	G, D
Anchorage (Zippy Branch)	215.3	
Aqua Yacht Harbor Marina	215.3	G, D
Anchorage (Panther Creek)	218.1	
Joe P. Coleman State Park Marina	220.0	G
Eastport Marina	224.5	G
Anchorage (Fish Trap Hollow)	224.5	
Anchorage (Ross Branch)	230.0	
Wilson Lock & Dam	259.4	
Steenson Marina	260.0	G
Anchorage	264.2	
Marina Mar Marina	264.7	G, D
Anchorage (Six Mile Creek)	266.0	
Doublehead Resort & Lodge	272.3	
Point Restaurant	272.3	G
Wheeler Lock & Dam	274.9	
Anchorage (Second Creek)	275.1	
Anchorage	275.8	
Joe Wheeler State Park Marina	277.0	G, D
Anchorage	277.0	
Anchorage	278.9	
Anchorage (Goldfield Branch)	285.1	
Lucy Branch Marina	287.0	G, D
Brickyard Landing Marina	303.7	G
Riverwalk Marina	305.0	G, D
Ditto Landing Marina	333.3	G, D
Anchorage (Flint River)	339.1	
Guntersville Lock & Dam	349.0	
Anchorage	349.5	
Anchorage (Honeycomb Creek)	351.5	
Alred Marina	357.4	G
Guntersville Marina	358.1	G, D
Signal Point Marina	358.5	G
Anchorage (Short Creek)	361.0	
Anchorage	361.7	
Goose Pond Colony Marina	378.0	G, D

Anchorage	378.0	
Anchorage	379.0	
Anchorage (Jones Creek)	388.0	
Nickajack Lock & Dam	424.7	
Anchorage (Shellmound)	425.5	
Hales Bar Marina	431.2	G, D
Chickamauga Lock & Dam	471.0	
Chickamauga Marina	471.4	G, D
Lake Shore Marina	471.7	G
Anchorage (Nance Hollow)	475.8	
Anchorage	476.2	
Island Cove Marina	477.5	G
Harrison Bay State Park	478.4	G
Anchorage (Dog Leg Slough)	478.4	
Anchorage (Huss Lowe Slough)	478.4	
Anchorage	483.3	
Pine Harbor Marina	487.5	G, D
Sale Creek Marina	494.7	G, D
Anchorage (Sale Creek)	494.7	
Anchorage	498.1	
Hiwassee River	499.4	
Anchorage	7.9	
Marina	12.9	
Blue Water Campground & Boat Dock	504.4	G
Watts Bar Lock & Dam	529.9	
Watts Bar Resort	530.4	G
Anchorage	530.4	
Anchorage (Lowe Branch)	531.0	
Rhea Harbor Resort & Marina	532.3	G
Anchorage (Pearl Harbor)	541.6	
Eden Resort Marina	542.3	G
Anchorage	546.7	
Anchorage	547.6	
Blue Springs Resort & Marina	547.7	G, D
Bayside Marina & Resort	548.2	G
Harbour Point Marina	551.0	G, D
Anchorage	558.2	
Anchorage	561.3	
Anchorage (Little Paint Rock Creek)	575.8	
Fort Loudoun Lock & Dam	602.3	

Tellico Lake

Anchorage	5.5	
Anchorage (Sinking Creek)	8.3	
Anchorage	18.1	
Tellico Harbor Marina	20.1	G
Anchorage	20.2	

Ft. Loudoun Marina	602.6	G, D
Concord Marina	616.1	G
Fox Road Marina	616.1	G
Anchorage (Sinking Creek)	616.1	
Anchorage	618.5	
Anchorage (Poland Creek)	620.2	
Anchorage (Caney Branch)	624.5	
PJ's Landing Marina	625.6	G
Travis Marine	626.9	
Duncan Boat Dock	635.2	G
Anchorage (Looney Island)	642.8	
Calhoun's Restaurant Dock	647.5	
Junction of Holston River and French Broad River	652.1	

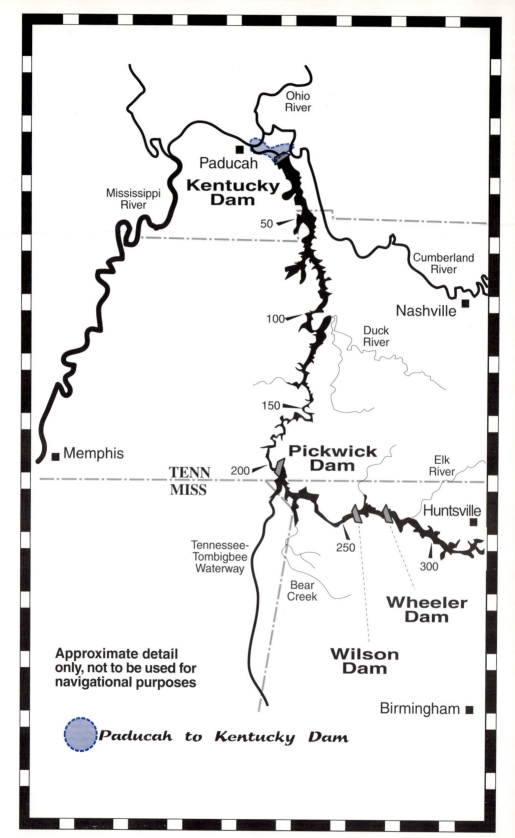

Ohio River

Paducah

Kentucky Dam

Mississippi River

50

Cumberland River

Nashville

100

Duck River

150

Memphis

Pickwick Dam

200

Elk River

TENN
MISS

Huntsville

Tennessee-Tombigbee Waterway

250

300

Bear Creek

Wheeler Dam

Approximate detail only, not to be used for navigational purposes

Wilson Dam

Birmingham

Paducah to Kentucky Dam

The
Tennessee
River

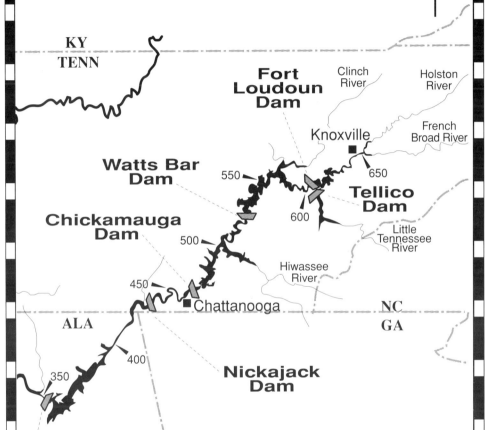

N

KY
TENN

Fort
Loudoun
Dam

Clinch
River

Holston
River

Knoxville

French
Broad River

Watts Bar
Dam

550

650

600

Tellico
Dam

Chickamauga
Dam

500

Little
Tennessee
River

450

Chattanooga

Hiwassee
River

NC
GA

ALA

400

Nickajack
Dam

350

Guntersville
Dam

Atlanta

MILE 0.0

Here, opposite Schultz Park at the foot of Jefferson Street in downtown Paducah, Kentucky, is where the Tennessee River empties into the Ohio River.

From here, you will increase your elevation by more than 500 feet as you travel the 652 miles upstream to where the Holston River and French Broad River join to form the Tennessee.

Paducah was founded in 1827 when General William Clark of the Lewis and Clark Expedition acquired the land and planned the town. He named the city in honor of Paduke, a peaceful chief of the Chickasaw Indian tribe who lived and hunted in the area.

The city is rich in history and historical structures. It has several attractions including the home and museum of U.S. Vice President Alben W. Barkley, the grave of humorist Irvin S. Cobb, and the new Museum of the American Quilter's Society. Bluegrass Downs, open since 1987, features American Thoroughbred Horse racing during October and November.

Paducah's riverfront is a mixture of trees, benches, and historic markers. Here, Clara Barton, founder of the American Red Cross, aided victims during the great flood of 1884. A wall now protects the city from floods such as the one in 1937 when almost the entire city was inundated.

Unfortunately for pleasure boaters, there are no marinas or established fuel sources at Paducah or between Paducah and Kentucky Dam which is 23 miles upstream.

Another important point is that heavy commercial tow traffic often causes long delays at the lock at Kentucky Dam. For that reason, you may want to consider the alternative of entering the Cumberland River at Ohio River Mile 923.0. After locking through Barkley Dam at Cumberland River Mile 30.6, you may then access the Tennessee through the free flowing canal that connects the two rivers just above Kentucky Dam. This alternate route, however, is about 17 miles farther if you are coming up the Ohio River from Cairo, Illinois.

For the first two miles after you enter the Tennessee at Paducah, the navigation channel is separated from the Ohio River by Owens Island at port. At starboard is a mixture of river related businesses and industries.

DAYMARK 2.0

This is the upper end of Owens Island where the Tennessee and the Ohio come together. You'll notice an increase in current as you pass through the narrow part of the river between Owens Island and Cuba Towhead at starboard. Here is where you turn to starboard around the upstream end of Cuba Towhead to begin your trip up the Tennessee.

For the next several miles, both sides of the river are lined with barges. Tow boat traffic tends to be heavy here, so stay alert.

MILE 5.3

This is the George Rogers Clark Memorial Bridge. U.S. 60 links several smaller towns with Paducah to the west and Henderson, Kentucky, and Evansville, Indiana to the east.

MILE 8.6

At starboard are the only riverside homes you will see between Paducah and Kentucky Dam. Few of them, however, have docks because of much more desirable boating conditions on Kentucky Lake.

DAYMARK 11.7

For about the next five miles, the river banks are uninhabited, low, and muddy. Streaks show previous high water levels. Here, the Tennessee looks more like a river than perhaps anywhere else along its entire length.

You are likely to see great blue herons in this area. These large and graceful birds often can be seen standing on the river bank or on a snag or swooping low over the water as they look for fish, frogs, or small reptiles.

DAYMARK 16.6

Across the river from this Daymark and for about the next three miles is the large industrial complex at Calvert City, Kentucky. Several industries, mostly manufacturers or processors of chemicals and metals, began locating here in the 1950s because of lower cost electrical power and river transportation.

MILE 20.0

Looking ahead, you will see the I-24 bridge. I-24 branches off I-57 in southern Illinois and extends to Chattanooga to provide a link between the Midwest and the Southeast.

MILE 22.4

Just beyond the bridge is Kentucky Dam. With a length of 8,422 feet, it's the longest of the nine main dams on the Tennessee. Construction began in 1938 and was completed in 1944.

The lock is on the east end of the dam. A railroad and U.S. highways 62 & 641 cross the river here.

If you must wait below Kentucky Dam, current may be a problem depending on how much water is being released. If several hours are involved, your best bet is to try anchoring close to the east bank at port and far enough downstream toward the I-24 bridge so as not to interfere with tows leaving the lock.

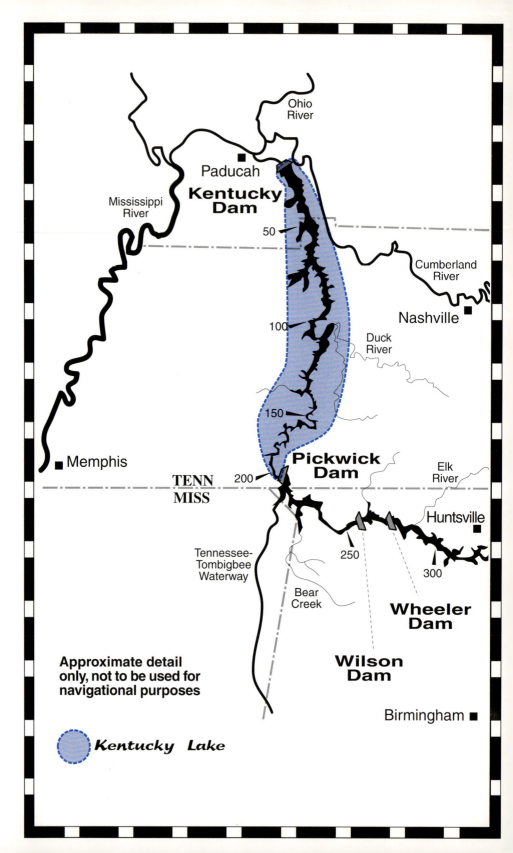

The *Tennessee River*

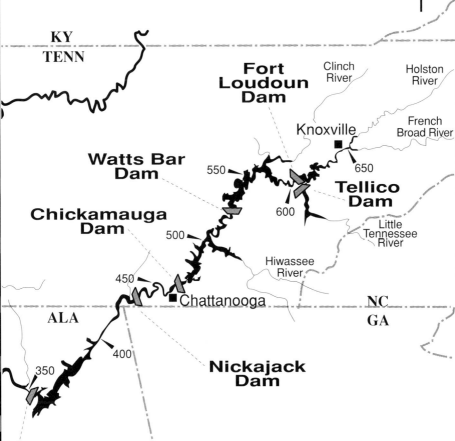

N

KY
TENN

Fort
Loudoun
Dam

Clinch
River

Holston
River

Knoxville

French
Broad River

Watts Bar
Dam

550

650

Tellico
Dam

600

Chickamauga
Dam

500

Little
Tennessee
River

450

Hiwassee
River

Chattanooga

NC
GA

ALA

400

350

Nickajack
Dam

Guntersville
Dam

Atlanta

The sweep of Kentucky Lake unfolds as you leave the lock at Kentucky Dam. A length of 184 miles and a shoreline of almost 2,400 miles make this one of the world's largest manmade lakes.

At the opposite end of the dam is the 1,200-acre Kentucky Dam Village State Resort Park. It has a full range of facilities including a lodge with dining room and an 18-hole golf course.

MILE 23.0
MARINA
RESTAURANTS
LODGING
ANCHORAGE

The park's marina is the largest in the Kentucky park system. If you look to starboard immediately after leaving the lock, you will see the roofs of the marina's slips in the distance. To reach the marina, follow the marked channel that parallels the dam to the opening in the rock breakwater.

Kentucky Dam Marina
P.O. Box 126
Gilbertsville, Kentucky 42044
502-362-8386

Open all year, 8AM until 7:30PM in summer, 8AM until 4PM in winter. Can accommodate boats to 90 feet. Water depth at the fuel dock is 15 feet at normal pool. Has 50 transient slips and 30 amp and 50 amp electrical service. Has gas and diesel fuel. Gas and diesel engine repairs are available. Has launch ramp, pump out station, ice, snacks, light groceries, and some marine supplies. A full range of groceries plus hardware supplies are available in Draffenville five miles away and a park courtesy car will take you there. Groceries also can be bought during the summer at the park's campground. Showers and laundromat are reached via park courtesy car. Monitors channel 16. Accepts MasterCard, Visa, and Discover credit cards.

Restaurants: The park lodge's dining room serves both from a menu and buffet. The park will provide transportation from the marina to the lodge.

Patti's in Grand Rivers, about a 20 minute drive, is an extremely popular gourmet restaurant famous for pork chops and pies. Adjoining Patti's and operated by the same family is Bill's. It shares many of the menu items and has an equally interesting environment. Reservations for both restaurants are strongly advised. A courtesy car will pick you up at the marina. Call 502-362-8844.

Lodging: The park lodge has 72 rooms plus efficiency and executive cottages. For more information call 502-362-4271 or 1-800-325-0143.

Anchorage: A marked secondary channel begins at the entrance to Kentucky Dam Marina and follows the west side of the lake to Mile 66.2 at Paris Landing State Park. Almost two miles up the channel and at the second red buoy is the wide entrance to the Sledd Creek embayment. It offers a water depth of at least 10 feet for most of its two-mile length. Except for a few houses on the north side, the embayment is surrounded by forest and farmland. Wind protection, especially from the south and west, can be good depending on where you anchor. There's plenty of space to swing on one anchor. The banks range from nearly level to moderately steep. Sledd Creek, however, can be busy on summer weekends. So if you're staying overnight, try to find a spot on the more secluded and protected south side.

Caution! The secondary channel and the channels that cross the lake to connect it with the main channel are well marked and safe to travel. But you must carefully follow the channel markers. This becomes even more important after the annual drawdown of water begins in July.

Two places offer the greatest potential for trouble when the water level is below normal pool. One is the cross channel connecting the main navigation channel at Mile 31.5 with the secondary channel at its Mile 7.0. It passes over the site of Birmingham, the only town inundated when Kentucky Lake was created. Many boats have been severely damaged as the result of hitting foundations and other remains of old buildings.

The second is at Mile 14.0 on the secondary channel. Here, the channel curves around an island. Stray outside these channel markers and you will suddenly be either in extremely shallow water or aground.

MILE 24.1
MARINA
RESTAURANTS
LODGING

Just above Kentucky Dam and upstream from the mooring cells, those large round steel structures for mooring tows, is Lighthouse Landing Marina. Two buoys and a large sign on top of the breakwater identify the entrance. Also, you'll see many sailboat masts in what is an unusually well protected harbor. This facility accommodates all kinds of pleasure craft but specializes in sailboats.

Lighthouse Landing Marina
P.O. Box 129
Grand Rivers, Kentucky 42045-0129
502-362-8201
E-mail: mcolburn@apex.net
Internet: www.lighthouselanding.com

Open all year, 8:30AM until 5:30PM from May to September, 9AM until 5PM for remainder of the year except closed on Sun-

day from December 1 until March 1. Can accommodate boats up to 45 feet. Has up to 10 transient slips with 30 amp electrical service. Water depth at fuel dock is 10 to 12 feet at normal pool. Has gas and diesel fuel. Has two launch ramps, showers, and laundry facilities on premises. Offers towing service, has 15-ton open end lift, and is exceptionally well equipped to handle all kinds of sailboat repairs plus rigging and stepping masts. Ship's Store offers nautical gifts, shoes, clothing and a wide range of boat parts and accessories. Rents and charters sailboats and offers sailing lessons. A complete line of groceries is available at a supermarket 2 blocks away in downtown Grand Rivers. Accepts MasterCard, Visa, and Discover credit cards.

Restaurants: See description of Patti's and Bill's at Mile 23.0. Both are two blocks away in downtown Grand Rivers and an easy walk from the marina. These restaurants, however, will send a courtesy car for you if you call them.

Lodging: Cottages at the marina have from one to three bedrooms. Reservations are required and none are taken for less than a two night stay.

DAYMARK 24.8
MARINA
RESTAURANTS
LODGING

Just beyond this Daymark is the entrance to the mile long free flowing Barkley Canal that connects Kentucky Lake on the Tennessee River with Lake Barkley on the Cumberland River.

If you planned to enter the Tennessee River via the Cumberland River you will be using this canal. In doing so, you will be coming past Green Turtle Bay which is between Barkley Lock & Dam and the canal. Or if you locked through Kentucky Dam and wish to visit this facility, enter the canal from Kentucky Lake, then turn to port after entering the Cumberland River. The entrance to Green Turtle Bay is less than a mile downstream at port. A marked channel extends through an opening in the breakwater and into the marina basin.

Green Turtle Bay Marina
P.O. Box 102
Grand Rivers, Kentucky
502-362-8364   Fax: 502-362-4119
E-mail: gtb@apex.net
Internet: www.kentuckylake.com\gtb\index.htm

Open all year, 8AM until 6PM Monday through Friday and 8AM until 8PM Saturday and Sunday April 1 until November 1, 8AM until 5PM remainder of year. Can accommodate boats up to 100 feet. Has 20 transient slips and 30amp and 50amp electrical service. Water depth at the fuel dock is 12 feet at normal pool. Has gas and diesel fuel. Has 25-ton and 60-ton lifts and can repair gas and diesel engines on both power and sail boats. Has showers, laundromat, pump out station, snacks, and well stocked ship's chandlery. Full grocery service is available one mile away in downtown Grand Rivers. Has courtesy car. Monitors channel 16. Accepts MasterCard, Visa, and American Express credit cards.

Restaurants: The restaurant on the premises is part of the Commonwealth Yacht Club. Although this is a private club, a courtesy card is available to transient boaters who stay overnight at the marina or are members of other yacht clubs registered with the Yachting Clubs of America.

Dockers, also on the premises, is a seasonal restaurant open April 1 until November 1 that serves breakfast and lunch.

Patti's and Bill's, see description at Mile 23.0, are about one mile away in downtown Grand Rivers. They will send a courtesy car to the marina to pick you up or you may use the marina courtesy car.

Lodging: Fifty fully equipped condos are a part of the marina complex and can be rented.

DAYMARK 25.4 ANCHORAGES

For about the next 40 miles, the entire east side of Kentucky Lake is known as the Land Between The Lakes or LBL. This spine of land up to eight miles wide separates Lake Barkley and Kentucky Lake and is one of the Nation's largest inland peninsulas.

LBL was created in 1963 by President Kennedy as a recreational and environmental education area. It has a special appeal to boaters because of its undeveloped shoreline; secluded coves; and wildlife including bald eagles, deer, and wild turkey.

Also at LBL is Empire farm which demonstrates a self-sufficient lifestyle, and the Homeplace, a farm home staffed by interpreters in period dress who do daily chores as they would have been done in the mid-1800s.

Within LBL are campgrounds, picnic areas, 200 miles of trails, and 300 miles of back country roads.

More than two dozen embayments indent the LBL shoreline. They provide excellent anchorages for overnight stays, swimming, and wildlife viewing. Water depth is nearly always more than adequate for large boats and there is plenty of space for swinging on one anchor. Campgrounds adjoin some of them but for the most part, there are no structures on the wooded banks. Wind protection will depend on where you anchor. These four embayments are especially appealing:

Pisgah Bay at Mile 30.1 is "L" shaped. The large cove to starboard soon after you enter is a particularly good area in which to anchor. At the entrance to the bay is a small splinter of land separating the bay from the site of an old stone quarry. Local boaters go there to escape sudden storms. But even in good weather, you may want to turn in here to see the colorful graffiti on the rock wall. Amazingly, almost all of it is in good taste. Along with dozens of examples of the "Debbie Loves Tom" variety, is evidence of genuine artistic talent.

Smith Bay at Mile 32.5 should be entered at the buoy on the upstream side to avoid shallow water on the north side of the entrance. This bay has a sand beach.

Duncan Bay at Mile 34.0 is another fine anchorage. The eastern half, however, is a waterfowl and eagle refuge and is off limits November 1 to March 15.

Sugar Bay at Mile 35.7 has a cove immediately to starboard as you enter that's particularly desirable. You will be protected from winds from almost every direction and have a fine view of the main lake.

Caution: Hydrilla and water milfoil are aquatic weeds that have spread to Kentucky Lake from upper reaches of the river to shallower water in some of the embayments. They can quickly become wrapped around propellers and plug generator intakes. Watch for these weeds and try to avoid them.

DAYMARK 29.1
RESORT
MARINA
RESTAURANT
LODGING

If you're looking for a resort rather than strictly marina atmosphere, you may wish to consider Moor's Resort & Marina. It can be reached by going 2.5 miles past Daymark 29.1 then turning to starboard on a marked channel that leads to the Bear Creek embayment. The marina is clearly visible as you approach the breakwater.

Moor's Resort & Marina
570 Moors Road
Gilbertsville, Kentucky 42044
1-800-626-5472

Open all year, 7AM until 8PM March 1 to November 1, resort office open 7AM until 8PM all year. Can accommodate boats up to 60 feet. The number of transient slips varies. Has 30 amp electrical service. Water depth at the dock is 13 feet at normal pool. Has gas. Has LP gas, ice, snacks, boating supplies, and a limited selection of groceries. Has showers and laundromat. Has a very low angle launch ramp. Monitors channel 16. Accepts MasterCard and Visa credit cards.

Restaurant: The Moors has a restaurant on the premises that serves home cooked meals and features buffets on weekends. It's open March 1 to December 1.

Lodging: Cottages at the Moors have from one to four bedrooms and can be rented by the day or week. A lodge has 24 hotel rooms plus a large meeting room.

MILE 41.9
MARINA
RESTAURANTS
LODGING
ANCHORAGE

The Eggners Ferry bridge carries U.S. 68 across the river. This highway connects Paducah and Benton to the west with the Land Between the Lakes, Cadiz, and Hopkinsville to the east.

The main and secondary navigation channels meet here. Then the secondary channel once again leaves the main channel. Follow it to starboard and you'll see Kenlake State Park.

The park has a lodge with dining room, a swimming pool, a 9-hole golf course, and an indoor-outdoor tennis center. To get to the marina, follow the red buoys into Ledbetter Creek to the entrance behind the rock breakwater.

Kenlake State Park Marina
888 Kenlake Marina Lane
Aurora, Kentucky 42048
502-474-2245

Open all year, 6AM until 8PM from May through October and 9AM until 3PM for the remainder of the year. Can accommodate boats up to 100 feet and has 10 transient slips and 30 amp and 50 amp electrical service. Water depth at the fuel dock is 11 feet at normal pool. Has gas and diesel fuel. Has launch ramp and can perform repairs on gas and diesel engines. Has snacks and limited selection of groceries. Park courtesy car will take you to the park lodge. Monitors channel 16. Accepts MasterCard, Visa, Discover, and American Express credit cards.

Restaurants: The restaurant at the marina is very popular with many local boaters and with returning transient boaters who have eaten there before. It serves breakfast and lunch from a general menu.

The park lodge's dining room serves both from a menu and buffet style. A park courtesy car will take you there.

Lodging: The park lodge has 48 rooms. Also available are cottages, some of which are efficiencies, with one to three bedrooms.

Anchorage: From the marina, continue up Ledbetter Creek past the park lodge. Behind the lodge is a large embayment with a depth of at least 10 feet at normal pool for about two-thirds of its length. There is plenty of space for swinging on one anchor. Although there are no structures, there is a highway at the end of the embayment. The wooded banks range from nearly level to moderately steep. You will be exposed to south and east winds but have a fine view of the lake.

DAYMARK 44.2
REPAIR FACILITY

Opposite Daymark 44.2 and on the west side of the lake is Harbor Hill Marine. It's on a small embayment between the secondary channel Daymark and the grain storage and shipping complex at the mouth of Anderson Creek.

Harbor Hill Marine
Route 3, Box 284B
Murray, Kentucky 42071
502-474-2228

Open all year, 7AM until 5PM. Largest repair facility on the Tennessee River between Pickwick Dam and Kentucky Dam. Water depth at fuel dock is 10 feet at normal pool. Has gas and diesel fuel. Has launch ramp and 50-ton lift to accommodate boats up to 60 feet. Offers towing service. Can service and replace generators, gas and diesel engines, and transmissions. Can repair and refinish metal, aluminum, and fiberglass. "If it has anything to do with boats, we can do it, have it, or can get it." Monitors channel 16. Accepts MasterCard, Visa, and American Express credit cards.

DAYMARK 50.9

A short distance upstream from this Daymark is one of the cross channels that connect the secondary channel with the main channel. If

49

you are cruising the secondary channel, consider joining the main channel now. The secondary channel beyond the Blood River embayment is narrow and tends to be too shallow for larger boats particularly if the water is below normal pool. If you do use the channel, go slow and be sure you stay between the channel markers.

By now, you have probably seen small boats with flat roofs and line and prongs dangling from frames. These boats arc used for harvesting mussels.

Mussels get their food by slightly opening their shells and filtering water. When the prong enters the opening, the mussel thinks it's a foreign object, clamps down on it, and doesn't let go until it's hauled into the boat. Undersized mussels are released.

Another way to harvest mussels is to dive and pick them up from the lake bottom. Small boats displaying the diver flag likely are being used by mussel harvesters.

The meat is used for fish bait. Most of the shells are exported to Japan where they are used either for mother of pearl jewelry or for seeding oysters for pearl production.

Each year, hundreds of tons of mussels worth more than a million dollars are harvested from the Tennessee River, mostly in Kentucky and Wheeler lakes.

DAYMARK 54.3 ANCHORAGE

Just before you reach this Daymark, you will see the entrance to Clay Bay. Water depth is at least 10 feet at normal pool for about three-fourths of the embayment's length. Because this area is still part of the LBL, you will be surrounded by wooded banks. There are no buildings, there's plenty of space on which to swing on one anchor, and you will be protected from all but west winds.

DAYMARK 62.6
ANCHORAGE

At this Daymark at starboard, you are leaving Kentucky and entering Tennessee.

Also, this is the beginning of the Cypress Creek embayment. Almost immediately after you turn up the creek, you will see a small cove at starboard. The water is at least 10 feet deep at normal pool for nearly all of its length. There's plenty of space for you to swing on one anchor. The area is wooded and there are no structures. The bank ranges from steep at the entrance to nearly level at the far end. This cove provides excellent wind protection and offers a fine view of the lake.

DAYMARK 64.4
MARINA
RESTAURANTS
LODGING

Less than two miles ahead is the Scott-Fitzhugh bridge. This is U.S. 79 which connects Paris to the west with the southern entrance to the Land Between the Lakes, Dover, and Clarksville to the east. The marked channel leading to Paris Landing State Park is at starboard just before you pass under the bridge and runs parallel to the bridge. You will see the fuel dock as soon as you enter the marina harbor.

The park was named after a landing established on the river in the mid-1800s. Freight was unloaded from steamboats and hauled in ox carts to nearby towns and communities.

The 841-acre park features a lodge with dining room plus an 18-hole golf course.

Paris Landing State Park Marina
16055 Highway 79 North
Buchanan, Tennessee 38222
901-642-4311 Lodge
901-642-3048 Marina Office

Open all year, 6:30AM until 8PM from March through October, 7AM until 5PM for remainder of the year. Can accommodate almost any size boat. Has 600 feet of walkway space for transient boats. Has 30 amp 110 volt and 50 amp 220 volt electrical service. Water depth at fuel dock is 14 feet at normal pool. Has gas and diesel fuel. Has ice. Laundromat (March through November) and showers are in camping area within walking distance. Has pump out station, snacks, and a few grocery items and boating supplies. Monitors channel 16. Accepts MasterCard, Visa, Discover, and American Express credit cards.

Restaurants: The park lodge's dining room a half mile away serves from a menu and also buffet style. If you don't care to walk, a park courtesy car will take you there.

There are several nearby restaurants that don't provide courtesy cars but are accessible by boat. Ask at the marina for directions for reaching them.

Lodging: The park lodge has 130 single and double guest rooms. The park also has 10 cabins that sleep up to 12 people.

MILE 67.0

A mile beyond the Scott-Fitzhugh bridge, the Tennessee is joined by the Big Sandy River. A marked deep water channel extends for six miles upstream.

DAYMARK 67.9

For the next five miles, all the water at starboard is included in one of Tennessee's National Wildlife Refuges. This refuge, one of three units along the river, totals 80,000 acres of water, woodland, and farmland.

Any farm or earth moving machinery you see working in this area is most likely being used to produce grain or to enhance water resources for use by wildlife.

In the fall, more than 150,000 ducks and 75,000 Canada geese arrive at the refuge for food and protection. Of the 23 species of ducks using the refuge, mallards are most common. So far, 226 species of birds have been identified on the refuge.

In summer, you are likely to see migrating shorebirds and wading birds such as the great blue heron along the exposed mud flats. Bald eagles and ospreys also spend the summer here but aren't seen as often.

From late August through September, Pace Point, where the Big Sandy River meets the Tennessee, is one of the best places in west Tennessee to see many kinds of shorebirds.

MILE 78.2

This is all that remains remains of the old L. & N. railroad bridge. Past the bridge at port is an abandoned dock that was an important shipping point on the Tennessee before Kentucky Dam was built.

For the next several miles, there is little to intrude upon the beauty of the water, wooded hills, and sky.

MILE 79.7
ANCHORAGE

Just past the red buoy is a marked channel leading to Bass Bay. Channel depth varies but won't be less than about 10 feet at normal pool. The channel is fairly straight for about a half mile then hooks sharply back to port before soon turning again to starboard and entering the embayment. The best place for anchoring is after you pass a small island and the last green buoy. Here, you'll find a wide area of water about 15 feet deep at normal pool. Except for a dock at starboard used by local fishermen and two distant launch ramps,

53

there are no structures. This is wide water and you will be exposed to wind from about every direction. In return, however, you will be rewarded with fine scenery and plenty of space in which to swing on one anchor.

**MILE 83.8
ANCHORAGE**

Getting into creeks and embayments suitable for anchoring is generally difficult along this stretch of the river. But Little Crooked Creek, the embayment at starboard, is an exception. Enter it downstream from the piling. At normal pool, water depth will be at least 10 feet across the embayment as you approach a point between the old and new launch ramps at starboard. This will allow you to anchor well away from the ramps and to swing on one anchor. There is only one house in the wooded surroundings and you will have a good view of the river. The banks are gently sloping to moderately steep. Wind protection is good from every direction except east.

DAYMARK 86.7

Several small islands ahead against a backdrop of distant hills help make this stretch of the river even more scenic.

DAYMARK 88.9

Soon after passing this Daymark, you will see the 600-foot stack at TVA's Johnsonville power plant. The nearby tanks and other facilities are part of an industrial complex.

DAYMARK 95.6

Across the river from the industrial facility is the Nathan Bedford Forrest Memorial State Park. The park marks the site of the Civil War battle of Johnsonville where Confederate forces led by General Forrest destroyed a Union supply depot. Pilot Knob in the park, named because of its use as a landmark by early steamboat pilots, is the home of the Tennessee Folklife Center.

For the next five miles, be particularly careful to stay inside the channel markers at starboard. Outside them the water becomes shallow very quickly.

MILE 100.5

Soon after passing the power plant you will pass under the Seaboard Systems railroad bridge. At normal pool, the lift span in the down position has a vertical clearance of 24.6 feet. If you need the bridge opened, call the bridge operator on channel 13 or 16.

On the other side of the bridge is the Hickman-Lockhart bridge. This is U.S. 70 which connects many small towns and communities north of I-40.

MILE 103.5
MARINA
RESORT
LODGING

At this point and just before you reach Daymark 103.7 is a sign on an island at starboard indicating Birdsong Resort & Marina. Immediately beyond is the mouth of Birdsong Creek. The well marked 2-mile channel leading to the marina has a depth of at least 10 feet at normal pool. Soon after you enter, the channel makes a tight loop to starboard, straightens, then curves slightly again before the creek widens considerably. At that point, you will see the marina ahead of you and the even more distant low clearance highway bridge. The fuel dock is near the middle of the marina.

Birdsong Resort & Marina
255 Marina Road, 1 Birdsong Place
Camden, Tennessee 38320-9699
901-584-7880
E-mail: birdsong@aeneas.net
Internet: www.birdsongresort.com

Open all year, dawn until dark with 24-hour security. Can accommodate boats up to 85 feet. Has six transient slips with 30 amp and

55

50 amp electrical service. Water depth at the fuel dock is 10 feet at normal pool. Has gas and diesel fuel, exceptionally wide and low angle launch ramp, and pump out station. Can do repair work on gas engines and has diesel mechanic on call. Has swimming pool, showers, laundromat, snacks, and boating supplies. A popular attraction on the premises is the fresh water pearl farm and pearl jewelry showroom. Rental cars and transportation to nearby restaurants and other services and to the Nashville Airport (85 miles) can be arranged. Monitors channel 16. Accepts MasterCard, Visa, Discover, and American Express credit cards.

Lodging: The resort has 11 fully equipped 1-4 bedroom housekeeping cottages. Reservations are suggested.

DAYMARK 103.7

Opposite this Daymark is a piling that marks the beginning of another unit of the Tennessee Wildlife Refuge. The refuge extends for several miles along the river.

At port, the shallow water is broken by thin slivers of low land covered with willows and some hardwood trees. Occasionally, you will see cypress trees along the edges of the river. They have small scalelike leaves that grow in dense fan-shaped sprays. Also, their trunks flare out at the base.

DAYMARK 106.2

Here, the river cuts into steep hills and exposes folds of yellow rock tinged with orange. This is the first evidence of what geologists call the Highland Rim, a large elevated and somewhat circular area that once covered most of central Tennessee. Most of the center, being of softer stone, has eroded. Only the harder rock remains. You are now passing through the western edge of the rim.

DAYMARK 109.3

The wide water at port is the mouth of Duck River. This river begins southeast of Nashville and flows westward for more than 200 miles across south central Tennessee. Only a few miles up Duck River is the mouth of the Buffalo River. Mostly fed by springs and flowing through countryside little changed from a hundred years ago, the Buffalo has gained a national reputation among canoists.

DAYMARK 111.1

In the distance is the I-40 highway bridge. I-40 begins in Greensboro, North Carolina, and ends in Barstow, California. It's the main highway linking such southern cities as Asheville, Knoxville, and Nashville to the east with Memphis, Little Rock, and Oklahoma City to the west.

MILE 115.5
MARINA
RESTAURANTS

Just after you pass Daymark 114.7 and about a mile before you get to the bridge you'll see Cuba Landing Marina in Blue Creek at port. Because of shallow water, don't try to enter this marina except via the marked channel at the upstream end of the small island.

Cuba Landing Marina
302 Cuba Marina Lane
Waverly, Tennessee 37185
931-296-2822
931-296-9756 (Fax)

Open all year, daylight until dark or later if necessary. Has seven transient slips plus space at the fuel dock for several more boats. Can accommodate boats up to 135 feet. Has 30 amp and 50 amp electrical service. Water depth at the fuel dock is 17 feet at normal pool. Has gas and diesel fuel. Has launch ramp and can do some mechanical repair. Has several grocery items. Has fresh deli during the summer months. Has snacks, ice cream,

57

ice, and boat supplies. Monitors channel 16. Accepts major credit cards.

Restaurants: There are four restaurants at exit #143 on I-40 about eight miles from the marina. The folks at the marina will give you more information and a courtesy car to use.

**MILE 125.0
ANCHORAGE**

This is Densons Island. The backside offers an anchorage with a water depth of about 30 feet at normal pool. To reduce anchor line scope, consider the alternative of anchoring near the river bank just below the island rather than directly behind it. The water is much shallower there and you will still be well away from river traffic. In either place, however, there are no structures to intrude upon the peaceful environment. Wind protection and swing room will vary depending on where you anchor.

DAYMARK 127.0

You are now passing through a landscape formed between 150 and 350 million years ago. Note the mostly gray limestone and shale ledges. All the rock you will see from here to the beginning of the Tennessee will be similar in appearance.

DAYMARK 130.2

At port is Lady Finger Bluff, a limestone bluff capped with gnarled cedar and hardwoods. Also here are fossil remnants of ancient marine life deposited when this part of North America was covered by a shallow sea. Legend has it that in pioneer days, a lady chose to leap to her death from this bluff rather than be caught by attacking Indians.

The river is narrower here than at any location since you left Paducah. In fact, this short stretch was known among early steamboat pilots as "the narrows." The water is from 70 to 80 feet deep as it moves in a slight curve between the bluff and the opposite bank.

DAYMARK 132.3

As you pass this Daymark, the Alvin C. York bridge comes into view. This highway, U.S. 412, is part of Tennessee's 2,300-mile Scenic Parkway System that leads to historical sites, state parks, attractions, and interesting out-of-the-way places.

MILE 135.0
MARINA
RESTAURANT

After you pass under the bridge, look to starboard for the sign indicating Michael's Perryville Marina. The channel leading to the marina is marked and although it may appear intimidating, water depth is about six feet at normal pool. Allow for wind and current as you approach the channel and try to stay close to center.

Michael's Perryville Marina
Route 1, Box 121
Parsons, Tennessee 38363
901-847-2444
1-800-850-3474

Open all year, 6AM until 7PM March through October, 6:30AM until 5PM for remainder of the year. Can accommodate boats up to 120 feet. Has six transient slips with 30 amp and 50 amp electrical service. Water depth at the fuel dock is about 10 feet at normal pool. Has gas and diesel fuel. Has launch ramp and offers repair service on gas engines. Has ice and some groceries. Arrangements can nearly always be made if you need to do major grocery shopping. Has snacks and a good selection of boat supplies. Monitors channel 16. Accepts MasterCard, Visa, and Discover credit cards.

Restaurant: The Scenic Restaurant, a mile away, has long specialized in catfish and steak dinners. It offers transportation to and from the marina.

MILE 140.0
MARINA
RESTAURANT

At starboard is a sign indicating the Gumdale Marina. The distance from the river to the marina office and fuel dock is less than 500 feet. Depth of the channel about eight feet at normal pool.

Gumdale Marina
110 Lagoon Lane
Decaturville, Tennessee 33829
901-852-2743

Open Monday through Friday, 9AM until 6PM, Saturday 8AM until 7PM, and Sunday from 8AM until 6PM from May 1 until the first weekend in November. At other times, phone ahead or call on the radio. Has seven transient slips with 30 amp and 50 amp electrical power and three slips without power. Has gas and diesel fuel. Has launch ramp. Has ice, snacks, light groceries and some boating supplies. A courtesy car is available. The Fisherdale Golf & Country Club, within walking distance, has an 18-hole course plus driving range. Monitors channel 16. Accepts MasterCard and Visa credit cards

Restaurant: The nearby Fisherdale Restaurant is open all year and offers sandwiches and short orders during the week and dinners on weekends.

MILE 143.0
ANCHORAGE

The water behind Kelley's Island has a minimum depth of about 25 feet at normal pool and offers good protection from west and southwest winds. It also will reward you with fine scenery dominated by fields to the east and the wooded slopes of Kittrell Ridge that drop sharply into the river upstream. The island has a low bank but the river bank here is moderately steep.

MILE 145.0

New Era Bluff at port consists of exposed

layers of limestone just as you saw back at Mile 127.0. The cedar trees clinging to these cliffs have little competition from other trees that can't tolerate the shallow and dry soil.

MILE 148.5 ANCHORAGE

Here, the navigation channel is between two islands identified on the official charts as Double Islands. On the smaller island at starboard is Daymark 149.1. Behind the larger island at port is an anchorage popular with area boaters. Water depth, about 25 feet at normal pool at the lower end, tapers to about 10 feet at the upstream end. Beyond the moderately steep river bank is a mixed landscape of trees and open fields. There are no structures and depending on where you anchor you will have good wind protection, especially from the east and west. There's plenty of space for swinging on one anchor.

MILE 152.5

You are now entering one of the sharpest hairpin turns on the Tennessee. You could leave the river here and return to it by traveling less than two miles across land, a distance that will require about nine miles by water.

MILE 155.0 ANCHORAGE

At starboard and across from the upstream end of Beech Creek Island is a long sand beach. Turn to starboard about half way between the red buoy and the beach. The water here will be about 15 feet deep at normal pool but ranges up to about 35 feet at normal pool after you pass the buoy. Even within a short distance of the beach, the water is too deep for easy anchoring. But continue to parallel the beach until you reach the far end. There, the water is only about 10 feet deep. You'll probably need both bow and stern anchors here but wind protection is excellent and only a few feet away will be one of the best sand beaches along this part of the river.

MILE 155.5

Here, the river again cuts through part of the Highland Rim to create impressive bluffs.

MILE 157.0

As you leave the curve, you will get your first glimpse of Clifton, Tennessee. Not since Paducah, Kentucky, 158 miles downstream, have you passed a town directly on the river.

At one time, Clifton was a major port. Part of its colorful history includes the story that when the vote was taken in 1843 to determine the location of Tennessee's capital, Clifton lost by only one vote.

Clifton's real claim to fame, however, is that it was the home of T.S. Stribling who won a Pulitzer prize in 1933 for his book, "The Store." The house in which Stribling lived can be seen from the outside but isn't open to the public.

MILE 158.5
MARINA
RESTAURANTS
LODGING

Just upstream from the old ferry landing and near the green buoy is the mouth of Roach Creek which is the entrance to Clifton City Marina. The narrow channel provides a water depth of about 4.5 feet at normal pool. Water in the embayment is slightly deeper and once inside you'll see the fuel dock at the far end.

Clifton City Marina
P.O. Box 634
Clifton, Tennessee 38425
931-676-5225

Open all year, 7AM until 8PM. Can accommodate boats up to 60 feet. Has no transient slips. Boats wishing to stay over-night can tie up to the fuel dock where water depth is about six feet at normal pool. Has gas. Has launch ramp. Repair facilities are off premises but close by. Has ice. A grocery and a bank are in downtown Clifton less than a mile away. Monitors channel 16. Accepts MasterCard and Visa credit cards.

Restaurants: A small restaurant inside the marina office building serves breakfast, lunch, and dinner. The menu ranges from sandwiches to plate lunches and steaks.

Katie's Country Cooking restaurant, about 1.5 miles east of Clifton, serves from a general menu but is best known for its catfish dinners.

Riverside Restaurant is about four blocks from the marina and is on the river. Although it serves a variety of dishes, catfish is the specialty. A view of the river is a bonus.

Lodging: The Clifton Motel is directly across the highway from Katie's Country Cooking restaurant. See the folks at the marina about possible transportation to both the restaurant and the motel.

MILE 161.9

This is the new Tenn. 60 bridge across the river that replaced the ferry at Clifton. The Highway links several area towns.

MILE 168.3
ANCHORAGE

At port is Indian Creek which forms the eastern border of Big River Plantation, a camping development. As you enter, stay in the center or slightly to port so as to miss a shoal that extends from the right bank. Water depth there will be about 11 feet at normal pool and decreases to about eight feet as you approach the point where the creek widens. This is a popular anchorage so you will probably feel more secure using both a bow and a stern anchor. The low banks range from open to wooded and there's good wind protection from every direction except north.

MILE 168.4

At starboard, you will be passing Swallow

Bluff Landing just before you reach Swallow Bluff. At one time, this was one of the busiest landings on the Tennessee. Such commodities as cotton and lumber were shipped from here.

MILE 171.8
FUEL

Inside the mouth of Doe Creek is a small sign indicating Scottie's Saltillo Marina. To get to the marina, you will be turning to port almost immediately after you enter the creek. If your boat is longer than about 40 feet, you may have difficulty in making the turn and in maneuvering near the marina. Water depth is about five feet at normal pool. You will especially welcome this stop if you need gas or if weather threatens. No fuel is available between here and Pickwick Landing State Park Marina at Mile 207.6, upstream from Pickwick Lock & Dam.

Ice, snacks, and light groceries are available. A grocery is about a half mile away in Saltillo. For more information, call 901-687-7353

MILE 172.3

This is the Saltillo ferry. It makes as many as 100 daily crossings. So be alert and reduce your wake to prevent interfering with its operation.

MILE 177.7

On your port side at this sharp bend, a road parallels the river for a short distance and leads into the community of Cerro Gordo. It was near here that the first white settlers arrived in 1816. A general store on the bluff, mostly hidden by trees, has been in business continually since the 1880s. At one time, cotton was loaded from the back of the building directly onto steamboats.

MILE 182.3

From here, you can see the large bluff ahead. The official charts identify this as Chalk Bluff, one of the most scenic and colorful on the lower Tennessee. But it isn't chalk. Rather, it's a mixture of sand and clay deposited many millions of years ago. Recent earth slides here are a reminder that despite man's attempt to control the river, it continues to change the landscape.

MILE 189.0

From here, you can see the Harrison-McGarity Memorial bridge which takes U.S. 64 across the river. This highway goes completely across the state and links many towns in the southern tier of counties. Also from here you will see the outskirts of Savannah, Tennessee.

Just before you pass under the bridge, note the two-story house with the square wood columns. This house, partly hidden by trees, is Cherry Mansion. It was built in 1830 on the site of prehistoric Indian mounds.

General Ulysses S. Grant was eating breakfast here on April 6, 1862, when he heard the distant dull thud of artillery fire as Confederate forces suddenly attacked his army at nearby Shiloh. The house continued to serve as Grant's headquarters during the fierce two-day battle.

MILE 192.0

The river banks here are low. The soil is a mixture of sand, clay, and gravel brought over the centuries by the river from farther upstream. Before dams were built on the Tennessee, all of what you see was often flooded by the raging river.

**MILE 195.3
ANCHORAGE**

This is Diamond Island. The navigation channel goes around the starboard side but the back side of the island offers good protection from river traffic and from all but north winds. To avoid shallow water and snags, stay to the center and don't go farther than about one-fourth of a mile. Water depth is about 25 feet at normal pool. The banks on both the island and the river are low to moderately steep. **65**

MILE 197.8

On your starboard side and just beyond the cleared area is the beginning of Shiloh National Military Park. It parallels the river for almost a mile. Unfortunately, there is no good place for you to tie up while visiting the park. But you will be able to get a few glimpses of the park through the trees.

Many visitors to the site say the Civil War becomes far more vivid to them here than at any other battlefield. Certainly, Shiloh is one of the most historically significant sites on the entire Tennessee River.

The battle of Shiloh, named after a church on the battlefield, was fought April 6-7, 1862. More than 103,000 Union and Confederate soldiers plus the Union gunboats TYLER and LEXINGTON were involved. By the time the battle had ended, 23,000 men were dead and dying. At such quickly named places as Bloody Pond, Hell's Hollow, and the Hornets' Nest, much innocence and enthusiasm was replaced by grim reality as those who had come to defend their cause discovered the horror of war.

DAYMARK 202.2

Caution! Here, the navigation channel narrows even more and the current increases. Although a channel widening project completed in 1996 has eased the situation, captains of large tows still must carefully maneuver to keep their tows between the channel markers and the river bank.

If you see a tow coming, slow down and immediately contact the tow captain on channel 13 or 16 for instructions on which side you should pass.

Another potential problem is where to stay if you are delayed in locking through. Anchor holding is poor because the channel bottom is mostly smooth rock. But it does improve somewhat as you move farther to port and closer to the launch ramp.

Because of turbulence caused by release of water from the main lock, don't try to tie up to the lower auxiliary lock wall. Also, erratic current makes it dangerous to attempt to tie up to the rings attached on the two steel encased mooring cells in mid-river.

As tedious as it will be, about your only alternative is to stay underway in the area until you can lock through.

MILE 206.7

This is Pickwick Dam. The dam is 113 feet high and 7,715 feet long. Construction was started in 1934 and completed in 1944. The highway that crosses the dam is Tennessee 128 which connects Iuka, Mississippi, with Savannah, Tennessee.

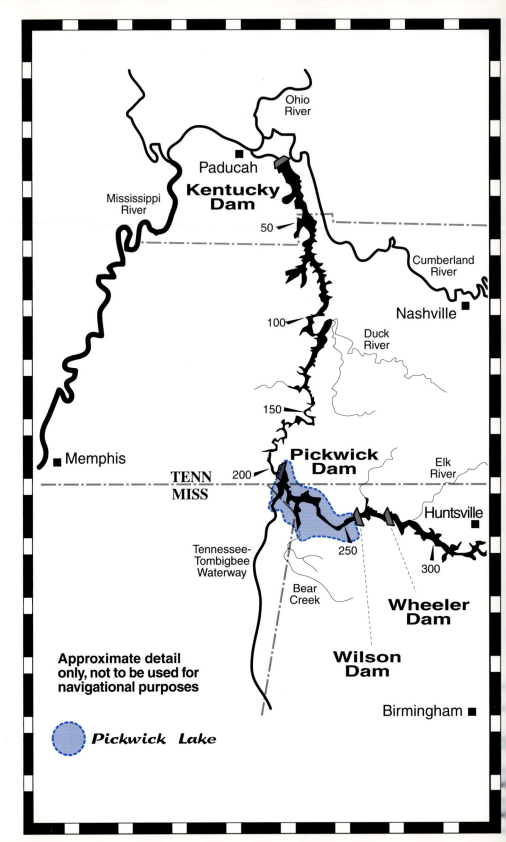

Ohio
River

Paducah

**Kentucky
Dam**

Mississippi
River

50

Cumberland
River

Nashville

100

Duck
River

150

Memphis

200 **Pickwick
Dam**

Elk
River

TENN
MISS

Huntsville

Tennessee-
Tombigbee
Waterway

250

300

Bear
Creek

**Wheeler
Dam**

**Approximate detail
only, not to be used for
navigational purposes**

**Wilson
Dam**

Birmingham

Pickwick Lake

The Tennessee River

N

KY
TENN

Fort Loudoun Dam

Clinch River

Holston River

Knoxville

French Broad River

Watts Bar Dam

550

650

600

Tellico Dam

Chickamauga Dam

500

Little Tennessee River

450

Hiwassee River

Chattanooga

NC
GA

ALA

400

Nickajack Dam

350

Guntersville Dam

Atlanta

As you leave the lock, you'll notice that the landscape has abruptly changed. The generally low banks and flat floodplain have been replaced by hills and cliffs. In fact, it was this sharp difference in topography that determined where Pickwick Dam was to be built.

Pickwick Lake draws boaters from a wide area including parts of Tennessee, Alabama, and Mississippi, plus such cities as Memphis and Nashville. Also, residential development has been rapid in recent years. As a result, the lower end of the lake is usually very busy on summer weekends.

MILE 207.6
MARINA
RESTAURANT
LODGING

Immediately upstream at the south end of the dam is Pickwick Landing State Resort Park. It was developed in 1969 around the old TVA Pickwick village. More than a thousand construction workers and their families lived here while Pickwick Dam was being built.

The resort complex includes a lodge with a restaurant and a golf course as well as a marina.

To reach the marina, turn starboard past the first buoy just beyond the two mooring cells above the lock. Follow the buoys to the embayment and continue past the launch ramp. Soon after you see the end of the sailboat dock, you will turn to starboard and continue straight ahead to the fuel dock.

Pickwick Landing State Park Marina
P.O. Box 10
Pickwick Dam, Tennessee 38365
901-689-3129 or 1-800-250-8615 Park Office
901-689-3135 Lodge
901-689-5175 Marina Office

Open all year, 6AM until 10PM. Can accommodate boats up to 60 feet. Has 10 transient slips with water and 30 amp and 50 amp

electrical service and 29 smaller slips without water and electricity. Water depth at the
fuel dock is 14 feet at normal pool. Has gas
and diesel fuel. Has launch ramp and ice.
Engine repair, LP gas, and boat store aren't
on the premises but are nearby. Has showers,
laundromat, and pump out station. If you
need groceries, a nearby grocery will pick
you up at the marina and bring you back.
Monitors channel 16. Accepts MasterCard,
Visa, and American Express credit cards.

Restaurant: The park lodge's dining room
can seat 150 and serves breakfast, lunch, and
dinner buffet style and from the menu. This is
a very popular restaurant, especially on summer weekends.

Lodging: The lodge has 75 single and double
rooms plus 3 suites. There also are 10 cabins
near the lodge.

DAYMARK 209.6
ANCHORAGE

Here, the river begins to turn sharply to the
south. While making the turn but before you
reach Daymark 212.6 at starboard, look for
the wide entrance to the large embayment on
the other side of the river. This is Dry Creek.
It extends about a mile inland from the main
lake. Water depth is at least 10 feet at normal
pool for about two-thirds of its length. There
are no structures, the wooded bank ranges
from flat to moderately steep, there's plenty
of space on which to swing on one anchor,
and you will be protected from all but northwest winds. There is, however, usually a lot
of boating activity here on summer weekends.

DAYMARK 215.3
MARINAS
RESTAURANTS
ANCHORAGE

This is where the Tennessee is joined by the
Tennessee-Tombigbee Waterway or
Tenn-Tom as it's usually called. It connects
the Tennessee with Mobile Bay on the Gulf
Coast 450 miles to the south. You are now

leaving Tennessee and entering Mississippi. Two marinas on the Tenn-Tom are often used by boaters cruising the Tennessee. One is Pickwick's Tenn-Tom Marina. It's clearly visible at starboard as you enter the Waterway. This marina is extremely vulnerable to wakes. So no matter if you are entering or just passing by, be conscious of your wake.

Pickwick's Tenn-Tom Marina
P.O. Drawer 1604
Pickwick Dam, Tennessee 38365
901-689-5551
901-689-5561(FAX)
1-888-689-5551
Internet: www.pickwickstenntommarina.com

Open all year, 24 hours a day. Can accommodate boats up to 70 feet. The number of transient slips varies. Has 30 amp and 50 amp electrical power. Water depth at the fuel dock is 18 feet at normal pool. Has gas and diesel fuel. Has launch ramp. Boat repairs can be arranged. Has ship's store, groceries, snacks, ice, showers and laundromat. Has courtesy car. Other services are being added at this marina. Monitors channel 16. Accepts all major credit cards.

Anchorage: About a half mile past Pickwick Cove Marina and on your port side is the Zippy Branch embayment. Water depth will be about 10 feet at normal pool for about two-thirds of its length. The wooded banks are gently sloping to moderately steep. The surrounding area is part of the Joe P. Coleman State Park. There are no structures. You will have plenty of space on which to swing on one anchor and be protected from wind from all directions. Keep in mind, however, that boating activity here is very high during summer weekends.

About two miles farther at the Tennessee-Tombigbee Waterway Daymark 448.7 on the upper end of an island, the navigation channel curves to port. But leave the Waterway here and bear to starboard. You will soon see Aqua Yacht Harbor Marina about a mile ahead. The long dock extending from the bank to the building is the transient dock. The fuel pumps are at the end of this dock which is marked by the cupola.

Effects of the wake you create here are deceptive. Unless you slow down even before you get to the no-wake buoys, you'll cause a lot of boats to bounce around, especially those on the transient dock. So take it easy.

Aqua Yacht Harbor Marina
3832 Highway 25 North
Iuka, Mississippi 38852
601-423-2222

Open all year, 8AM until 5:30PM but keeps later hours during the summer. Can accommodate boats up to 125 feet. Has 25 transient slips and 30 amp and 50 amp electrical service. Water depth at the fuel dock is 20 feet at normal pool. Has gas and diesel fuel. Has launch ramp. Has 70-ton lift and complete facilities for gas and diesel engine and fiberglass repair and for servicing and repairing both powerboats and sailboats. LP gas is available off premises. Has showers, laundromat, pumpout station, snacks, some boating supplies, and light groceries. Full grocery service is available in and near Counce, Tennessee, five miles away, and can be reached by courtesy car. Transient boaters may use the swimming pool, tennis court, and exercise facilities on the premises. Monitors channel 16. Accepts MasterCard, Visa, Discover, and American Express credit cards.

73

Restaurants: Cafe St. Clair on the premises serves light foods and full dinners from a menu.

Nearby restaurants specialize in catfish, barbeque, and pizza. Some will pick you up at the marina or you can use the marina courtesy car.

DAYMARK 218.1
ANCHORAGE

As you pass this Daymark, look across the river and you'll see the mouth of Panther Creek. Water depth will be about 18 feet at normal pool until you reach the point where the embayment splits. If you turn starboard and go past the boat launch and the clump of small cypress trees, the embayment widens somewhat and water depth will be at least 10 feet for some distance. You will have plenty of space to swing on one anchor and good wind protection from every direction except west.

For even greater wind protection, turn to port at the split. Favor the steep bank at port where you will have a water depth of about 12 feet. The water quickly becomes more shallow as you move farther into the embayment or to starboard. Because this is a state wildlife management area, the nearly level to moderately steep banks are wooded and there are no structures. Also from either location, you will be able to enjoy a view of the main lake. On both land and water, the Panther Creek area can get busy on summer weekends. But because this is one of the best anchorages on Pickwick Lake, it's still worth considering.

MILE 220.0
FUEL

Here at the mouth of Indian Creek is the Joe P. Coleman State Park Marina. To reach the fuel dock, turn immediately to port as soon as you pass the no wake buoys and go to the end of the first covered dock.

This facility is open May through October, 10AM until 5PM weekdays, except closed on Monday and Tuesday, and 9AM until 5PM on weekends. Has gas, ice, and launch ramp. Monitors channel 16. For more information, call 601-423-6515.

DAYMARK 224.5 MARINA ANCHORAGE

Beyond this Daymark and at starboard is the mouth of Bear Creek. The water is so wide here that some boaters have made the mistake of thinking it was the Tennessee.

Soon after you make the turn into Bear Creek you will see the sign at starboard indicating the entrance to Eastport Marina. The fuel dock is at starboard after you pass three docks with covered slips.

Eastport Marina
892 County Road 956
Iuka, Mississippi 38852
601-423-6972

Open all year, 7AM until 5PM Sunday through Thursday and 7AM until 7PM Friday and Saturday May through September, and 8AM until 5PM Tuesday through Saturday, October through April. Has five transient slips and 30 amp and 50 amp electrical service. Water depth at the fuel dock is 20 feet at normal pool. Has gas. Repair on gas engines is available. Has launch ramp, showers, snacks, sandwiches, and a few boating supplies. Monitors channel 16. Accepts MasterCard and Visa credit cards.

Anchorage: Fish Trap Hollow is up Bear Creek about a mile beyond Eastport Marina, on the same side, and beyond the houses. Near the entrance, some of the vertical bank has a white chalky appearance. A water depth of about 15 feet at normal pool begins about two-thirds up the embayment. The area is wooded and there are no structures. The bank ranges from level to very steep. This anchorage offers excellent wind protection from all directions except east and there is plenty of space for you to swing on one anchor.

DAYMARK 226.6

The concrete structure on which this Daymark is installed is the only visible evidence of the old Riverton lock, part of what once was a canal and lock system built more than 100 years ago. A canal extended upstream for about five miles so boats could bypass rapids and shoals. It was covered by water when Pickwick Dam was closed.

Across the river is Waterloo, Alabama, founded in 1832 by settlers from the Carolinas. It's one of the state's oldest incorporated areas and has almost met its "Waterloo" three times. Most of the town had to be rebuilt after a disastrous flood in 1844. A few years later, its fate hung in the balance when General Sherman's army headquartered here during its march through the South. Then in the 1930s, the town, except for some of the more stately homes originally built on higher ground, had to be moved when Pickwick Dam was built. Today, Waterloo is a quiet community with a population of about 300. There are no docking facilities for large boats.

Beyond Waterloo the river flows through several miles of a rural and mostly wooded landscape.

MILE 230.0
ANCHORAGE

This is Ross Branch, the last good anchorage until after you enter Wilson Lake at Mile 259.4. Because of the surrounding hills, it's also an ideal place to wait out a thunderstorm. Enter between the two rock piles closest to the navigation channel. Soon after you pass a second rock pile at port, water depth suddenly drops from about 15 feet at normal pool to about 30 feet then quickly rises again to about 15 feet. This is because you have just passed over the old canal that at one time skirted the river.

As you approach the white crosses on the bank, water depth will decrease rapidly. So go slow and keep close watch on your depthfinder. The moderately steep wooded banks have no structures, there's plenty of space for you to swing on one anchor, and you'll have excellent wind protection from every direction except north.

MILE 233.0

After Daymark 231.4, the river takes a more southerly course and by the time you reach this point you will be able to see the mile-long Natchez Trace Parkway bridge. Completed in 1965, it's architecturally one of the most graceful bridges spanning the Tennessee.

During the early 1800s, George Colbert, an enterprising Chickasaw Indian, lived on a hill overlooking the river and operated a ferry near what is now the west end of the bridge.

The 450-mile long Parkway is part of the National Park System and closely follows the route of the historic Natchez Trace.

The Trace began as an Indian trail and was discovered by the French sometime before 1733. It extended from Natchez to Jackson, Mississippi, then northeastward to Nashville, Tennessee. Later, the trail was used by traders, missionaries, and soldiers.

About 1785, men from Ohio, Kentucky, and other parts of the frontier began using flatboats to deliver products down the Mississippi River to Natchez and New Orleans. Once downriver, they sold the boats for lumber and used the Trace for the overland trip back home. The Trace was traveled by many notables including John James Audubon, Meriwether Lewis, and Andrew Jackson.

Use of the Trace dropped sharply then ended when travel by steamboat was introduced. But as the years passed, the Trace became so historically significant that in 1934, Congress authorized a survey to determine possible construction of a parkway. The project was eventually approved.

Now, the Trace provides motorists with a leisurely and scenic route with many picnic areas, nature trails, exhibits, and points of interest. In some places ruts of the original trace can still be seen.

About two miles beyond the bridge at port is Kogers Island. Beginning here and for the next 15 miles pay close attention to the channel buoys. At normal pool, the water hides rocks, stumps and mud banks that give headaches to careless boaters.

MILE 245.0

This is TVA's Colbert power plant, one of several coal burning plants operated by TVA to produce electricity.

MILE 247.0

At port is the downstream end of Seven Mile Island. The island has long interested archeologists because it was the site of several Indian villages. Many artifacts have been found on the island. Unfortunately, however, many others have been removed illegally. Removing archeological or biological resources on all TVA lands is against the law.

Beginning here, the river becomes much narrower. The closeness of the bank on one side and the small and low lying islands on the other create a different feeling than what you experienced a few miles downstream.

DAYMARK 251.6

You are now entering the Muscle Shoals area. It consists of four cities and is the third largest urban area through which the Tennessee River passes. Only Chattanooga and Knoxville are larger.

Florence, largest of the four cities and at port on the north side of the river, was laid out in 1818 by Ferdinand Sannoner. The Italian surveyor was given the honor of naming the new city. He chose Florence after Florence, Italy, where he had lived.

The other three cities are on the south side of the river. Muscle Shoals was incorporated in 1923. It was the result of a land boom following Henry Ford's announcement in 1921 that he intended to build a 75-mile long city and giant industrial complex at the site. Although Ford's dream never materialized, the city has become an important retail center.

Sheffield was founded in the 1880s by a small group of wealthy businessmen who envisioned it becoming an iron and steel center. Named after Sheffield, England, also a steel center, the city thrived on the industry into the 1920s.

Tuscumbia, incorporated in 1820, was named after a locally prominent Chickasaw chief. Other than Boston, Massachusetts, it's the only U.S. city to have a Commons. It was here in 1832 that the first railroad west of the Appalachian Mountains was built.

The four cities have a combined population of about 75,000 and offer several attractions for visitors including the homes of two world famous personalities, W.C. Handy and Helen Keller. Annual festivals honor them.

Handy, "Father of the Blues", was born in Florence. His home is now a museum that contains such momentos as his trumpet and the piano he used to write many of his songs including "The St. Louis Blues."

Said Handy, "If my serenade of song and story should serve as a pillow for some composer's head, yet perhaps unborn, I will not have labored in vain. If, as my teacher predicted, music brought me to the gutter, I confess it was there I got a glimpse of Heaven, for music can lift one to that state."

Helen Keller became blind and deaf soon after being born in Tuscumbia in 1880. Yet, she overcame those handicaps to become known throughout the world as a writer, philosopher, and speaker. She was often called the "First Lady of Courage."

Her story was told in a 1962 film, "The Miracle Worker." Patty Duke and Anne Bancroft won Oscars for their performances in the film. The Keller home, including the famous pump where Helen learned to say "water," is open to the public.

MILE 255.0

The fishing pier at the mouth of Cypress Creek is the west end of McFarland Park. Included in the park is an 18-hole golf course.

At the other end of the park is a harbor providing a water depth of about 10 feet at normal pool. The Florence Harbor Marina is scheduled to be built at this location. Call 256-740-4141 for the latest information on the progress of this development.

Just beyond the park is O'Neal Bridge. This is U.S. 72 which connects Florence with Muscle Shoals, Sheffield and Tuscumbia. It's also the principal highway linking these cities with Memphis to the west and Huntsville and Chattanooga to the east.

As you pass under O'Neal Bridge you will enter the navigation channel that swings slighty to port as it parallels the main river and leads to Wilson Dam.

The old railroad bridge at starboard was built in 1839 and is one of the most historic structures on the Tennessee. The lower deck was used by pedestrians, people on horseback and wagon traffic. Severely damaged by a tornado in 1854, the bridge was rebuilt by the Memphis & Charleston Railroad to accommodate steam-powered trains.

In 1862, the bridge was partly destroyed by a fire set by Confederate troops attempting to halt advancing Union forces. The bridge was rebuilt again and in 1893 a new steel superstructure was added. Twelve years later an electric street car system was installed on the top deck while automobiles began using the lower deck.

After O'Neal Bridge was completed in 1939, the bottom deck was removed, leaving the top deck for trains which used the bridge until rail service ended in 1988. In 1993, the lift section over the navigation canal was removed and soon afterward the entire bridge was threatened with demolition. A private group, however, gained title to the bridge. It plans to restore the bridge and convert it into a pedestrian walkway that will extend to the Patton Island Natural Reserve.

MILE 259.4

This is Wilson Dam, one of the most significant structures on the Tennessee River. The dam is 137 feet high and 4,541 feet long.

Named after Woodrow Wilson, the 28th president of the United States, the dam is the oldest on the river. Construction began in 1918. At its peak, the project involved more than 18,000 workers. An average of 111 railcar loads of equipment and materials arrived daily and more than 800 bricklayers worked at one time under a single roof. When the dam was completed in 1925, it was heralded as the world's largest.

The dam is architecturally intriguing. The arches forming the spillways are patterned after construction skills dating back to the Roman Empire. In 1966, the U.S. Department of Interior designated the dam a National Historic Landmark. The highway on top of the dam is Alabama 133.

There are two sets of locks at Wilson Dam. Nearest the bank is the original and small two-chamber lock. It has been rebuilt but is used only in emergencies or when the main lock is closed for repair.

The new lock and the one you will be using was built in the 1950s. At one time it was the world's highest single lift lock. It now ranks third behind a lock on the Snake River in Washington State and another in Eastern Europe.

If you must wait below the lock, a convenient and safe place to do it is along the lower wall of the old lock. It offers several recessed and easily reached mooring posts for tying off. Also, because water from the main lock is released into the main river on the other side of the lock, the water in this area is free of turbulence.

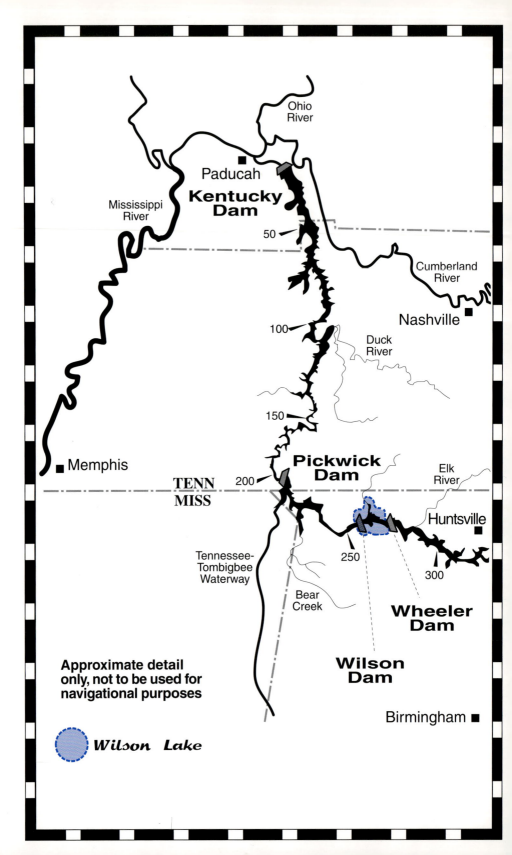

Ohio River

Paducah

Kentucky Dam

Mississippi River

50

Cumberland River

Nashville

100

Duck River

150

Memphis

Pickwick Dam

Elk River

TENN

200

MISS

Huntsville

Tennessee-Tombigbee Waterway

250

300

Bear Creek

Wheeler Dam

Wilson Dam

Approximate detail only, not to be used for navigational purposes

Birmingham

Wilson Lake

The
Tennessee
River

N

KY
TENN

Fort
Loudoun
Dam

Clinch
River

Holston
River

Knoxville

French
Broad River

Watts Bar
Dam

550

650

Tellico
Dam

600

Chickamauga
Dam

500

Little
Tennessee
River

450

Hiwassee
River

Chattanooga

NC
GA

ALA

400

Nickajack
Dam

350

Guntersville
Dam

Atlanta

With a length of only 15 miles, Wilson Lake is the shortest of all the lakes on the Tennessee. It's also one of the deepest with water depths as great as 125 feet.

The fall in the river was greater in this part of the Tennessee than anywhere else along the entire river. The river bed beneath you is a mass of rocks so jumbled that before Wilson Dam was built, the river's roar during times of flood could be heard up to a mile away. A canal and lock system that skirted the north bank to route boats around the rapids is now covered with water.

There are perhaps more private homes per mile along Wilson Lake than on any other lake. The reason is that when Wilson Dam was closed in 1924, land along Wilson Lake continued to be privately owned. But as TVA, established ten years later, began building the other dams on the Tennessee, it retained control of most of the land bordering the water.

MILE 260.0
MARINA

At the far end or south end of the dam and not visible as you leave the lock is an embayment containing commercial docks plus a large launch ramp. The second large embayment upstream from that point is Steenson Hollow at the end of which and at starboard is Steenson Marina.

Steenson Marina
P.O. Box 281
Sheffield, Alabama 35660
256-383-7859

Open 9AM until 5PM March through October. Call ahead for remainder of the year. Can accommodate boats up to 50 feet. Overnight dockage can be provided but utilities may not be available. Water depth at the fuel dock is 15 feet at normal pool. Has gas, launch ramp and 35-ton open end lift. Major repairs by appointment only. Monitors channel 16 during season. Accepts MasterCard and Visa credit cards.

MILE 263.0

The large embayment at starboard is identified on the official charts as McKernan Creek but is known locally as Donnegan's Slough. This may be of interest if you wish to do some leisurely sightseeing of lakefront homes or take a break from traveling on the main lake. When you enter, however, favor the upstream side to avoid shallow water and underwater obstructions.

MILE 264.2
ANCHORAGE

Because of Wilson Lake's small size, the surrounding topography, and population density, ideal anchorages don't exist. But this is the first of the two best ones. A mile beyond Donnegan's Slough is a long and narrow embayment. Water depth is at least 25 feet at normal pool for most of its length. Not until you approach the far end where water depth is about 10 feet at normal pool is it shallow enough for easy anchoring. Even then, you will probably need a stern anchor because swinging room is limited. You will have excellent protection from winds from any direction. The wooded banks are moderately steep. Unfortunately, however, development continues to intrude on this formerly secluded area.

DAYMARK 264.7
MARINA
RESTAURANT
FOOD
LODGING

From here on a clear day, you can see both Wilson Dam almost five miles downstream and Wheeler Dam ten miles farther upstream. Directly across the river is the mouth of Shoal Creek.

Less than two miles up Shoal Creek and at port just before you reach the U.S. 72 bridge, is Marina Mar. When you enter Shoal Creek, favor the downstream side to avoid shallow water at starboard which is marked with a buoy. Be particularly alert here on summer weekends when boat traffic is heavy on Shoal Creek and in the immediate area of the lake.

Marina Mar
4424 Highway 72 East
Florence, Alabama 35634
256-757-1122
Riverchase Boat Sales & Service
256-757-4115

These two businesses operate on the same premises but have different functions. Arrangements for transient slips are made through Marina Mar. Riverchase provides all other services.

Open all year, 8AM until 6PM May through August, 9AM until 5PM for remainder of the year. Can accommodate boats up to 65 feet in open slips and up to 40 feet in covered slips. Number of transient slips varies. Has 30 amp and 50 amp electrical service. Water depth at fuel dock is 12 feet at normal pool. Has gas and diesel fuel. Launch ramp is nearby but not on premises. Has ice, showers, and ship store. Rental cars are available. Monitors channel 16. Accepts MasterCard, Visa, Discover, and American Express credit cards.

Restaurant: The Galley, a restaurant on the premises, is open 7:30AM until 9PM daily and serves breakfast, sandwiches, and dinners. The restaurant has two slips for small boats but larger boats must tie up to the long dock perpendicular to the fuel dock.

Food: Several establishments will deliver food to the marina. Check with the folks at the marina for details.

Lodging: A Super 8 Motel is nearby at the east end of the Shoal Creek bridge. For more information, call the motel at 256-757-2167.

The fixed twin span U.S. 72 bridge immediately beyond the marina has a vertical clearance of 14.6 feet at normal pool. Smaller boats can safely venture up Shoal Creek for about three miles past the bridge.

After you return to Wilson Lake and turn upstream, the private Turtle Point Golf & Country Club will be at port.

MILE 266.0 ANCHORAGE

After passing Daymark 265.0 look across the river to spot Six Mile Creek, the second good anchorage on Wilson Lake. Although sometimes difficult to see, the wide mouth of the creek becomes much more apparent as you approach it. To avoid shallow water and possible snags, enter this embayment only on the upstream side. Continue to favor your starboard side until you are near where the creek turns abruptly to starboard. Water depth there will be about 15 feet at normal pool and there's enough space for swinging on one anchor. Wind protection is good from almost every direction. The creek, however, is busy on summer weekends.

DAYMARK 268.9

You'll notice on the official charts that directly across from this Daymark and slightly more than half way across the lake is a shallow area. Photographs made before Wilson Dam was built show this as a hill high enough to be considered a local landmark. At low water, it can be a hazard for larger sailboats and deeper draft power boats.

DAYMARK 272.3 RESORT RESTAURANT FUEL

As you near this Daymark at port, look to starboard and you will see two pile structures that mark an extremely shallow area. Beyond the upstream structure is the marked entrance to Town Creek. Although much of this embayment is shallow, the channel is deep and well marked.

Caution! The aerial power crossing has a vertical clearance of 36.5 feet at normal pool.

As the main channel curves to starboard, a marked secondary channel at port leads to Doublehead Resort & Lodge which can be seen in the distance. Water depth will be at least six feet at normal pool. Be sure to stay well within the channel markers. The channel is fairly straight for about a half mile then curves to port around the point to the six transient slips behind the lodge. The slips can accommodate boats to 60 feet and have 30 amp and 50 amp electrical power.

This new resort is unique because it lies within a privately owned 1,100-acre wildlife preserve. Named after Doublehead, the legendary Cherokee Indian chief who lived on the site, it's an excellent location for spending a few days off the boat or to rendezvous with friends. It features 35 fully furnished cabins with three bedrooms and two baths, convenience store and gift shop, conference center, white sand beach, swimming pool, horseback riding and sporting clays. Quail, pheasant, and chukar hunting is offered in season. For more information and reservations write to Doublehead Resort & Lodge, 145 County Road 314, Town Creek, Alabama 35672 or call 1-800-685-9267.

The main channel continues to curve to starboard to the Point Restaurant. It serves seafood Thursday, Friday, and Saturday evenings and Sunday beginning at noon. Gas is available 7AM until 7PM, April to October, and during winter depending on the weather. For more information call 256-466-6880.

MILE 272.6

Beginning here, buoys mark both sides of the navigation channel as it approaches the lock at the north end of Wheeler Dam.

Bluewater Creek at port is sometimes used by local boaters caught on the lake during sudden summer storms. Also, you might choose to wait here if you face a long delay in getting through Wheeler Lock. If you do enter the creek, stay on the downstream side and well off the buoys that indicate shallow water and the underwater remains of the old canal and lock system used before Wilson Dam was built. At normal pool, water depth will be at least six feet for the first few hundred feet up the creek.

MILE 274.9

This is Wheeler Dam. It was named for Joseph Wheeler, a West Point graduate. He was a general in the Confederate Army and a leader of U.S. volunteers in the Spanish-American War. During his military career, General Wheeler fought in more than 500 skirmishes, commanded in 127 battles, had 36 staff officers wounded at his side, and had 16 horses shot from underneath him. Elected to Congress in 1880, Wheeler died in 1906 and was buried in Arlington Cemetery. His home was built in 1872 a few miles south of the dam and is an important historical structure.

Only 72 feet high, Wheeler Dam is the lowest of all the dams on the Tennessee. But with a length of 6,342 feet, it's the third longest. Construction began in 1933 and was completed in 1936.

If the lockmaster requests you to use the auxiliary lock, note that there are only four floating mooring posts, one on each side as you enter and one on each side at the far end.

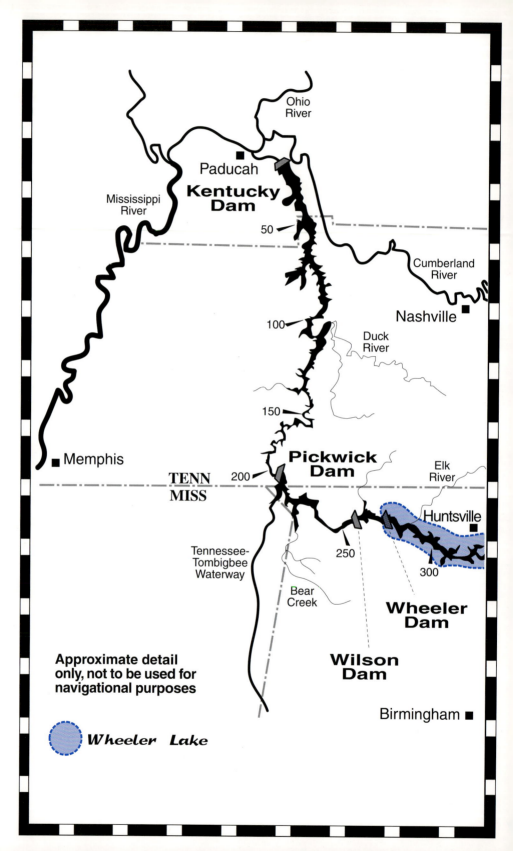

The Tennessee River

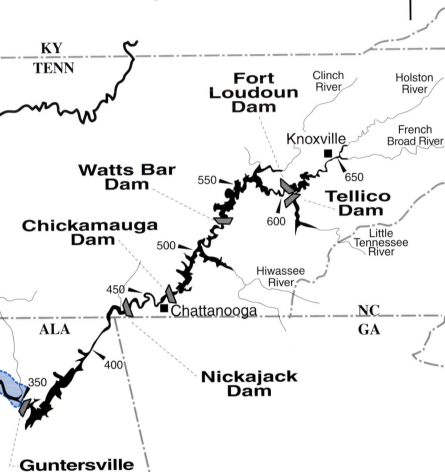

N

KY
TENN

Fort Loudoun Dam

Clinch River

Holston River

Knoxville

French Broad River

650

Watts Bar Dam

550

600

Tellico Dam

Chickamauga Dam

500

Little Tennessee River

450

Hiwassee River

400

Chattanooga

NC
GA

ALA

Nickajack Dam

350

Guntersville Dam

Atlanta

Ahead of you, at least for a few miles, is some of the widest water on the entire river. It's also comfortably deep from bank to bank.

MILE 275.1
ANCHORAGE

Immediately to port as you leave the lock is the entrance to Second Creek. This embayment is about two miles long and is a good place to get away from the main river. It is, however, a favorite with local boaters on summer weekends.

A good anchorage is an embayment at port about three-fourths of a mile up Second Creek past three small coves and before the creek turns. The best place to anchor is just before the embayment splits. Water depth will be about 12 feet at normal pool and there's plenty of room to swing on one anchor. Wind protection is good from every direction. There are no structures and the nearly level to moderately steep banks are wooded.

DAYMARK 275.8
ANCHORAGE

If you want a more convenient anchorage where you will have a good view of the main lake, turn to port soon after passing this Daymark. The best location will be a short distance before the embayment splits. Water depth is about 10 feet at normal pool and there's plenty of space to swing on one anchor. The gently sloping banks are wooded and you will be protected from all but a south wind. An option is the small embayment at port where water depth is about 20 feet at normal pool. This provides good protection from west and southwest winds during sudden thunderstorms.

MILE 277.0
MARINA
RESTAURANT
LODGING
ANCHORAGE

About two miles above the dam at port is Joe Wheeler State Resort Park. Among the facilities offered by this complex are a lodge with a dining room and a golf course.

94

The lodge and marina aren't on the main river. To reach them, turn into the wide mouth of First Creek. A large sign there identifies the park. After a short distance, you will turn to starboard and the lodge and marina will be directly ahead of you.

The dock in front of the lodge is used for transient boats and is nearly always filled to capacity on summer weekends. The number of remaining transient slips varies and consists mostly of covered slips. No reservations are taken but it sometimes helps if you call the marina early on the same day of your planned arrival.

Joe Wheeler State Park Marina
P.O. Drawer K
Rogersville, Alabama 35652
256-247-5461 (Lodge)
256-247-6971 (Marina)

Seasonal operation. Open 7AM until 6PM Monday through Friday, 7AM until 7PM on Saturday and Sunday, from May 1 to November 1. Closed November 1 to March 1 but fuel is available by calling 256-247-5466. Can accommodate boats up to 65 feet. The number of transient slips varies. Has 30 amp and 50 amp electrical service. Water depth at the fuel dock is 20 feet at normal pool. Has gas and diesel fuel. Has launch ramp, ice, light groceries, showers, laundromat, limited boating supplies, and pump out station. Monitors channel 16. Accepts MasterCard, Visa and American Express credit cards.

Restaurant: The lodge's dining room overlooks First Creek and the marina and offers a variety of dishes from a menu plus buffet service on weekends.

Lodging: The lodge has 74 units including nine suites. There also are 23 rustic cabins.

Anchorage: An alternative to docking at the marina is to anchor on the opposite side of First Creek in the wide part through which you passed enroute to the marina. Anchor as close to the far bank as you can and as water depth permits so you will be as far out of the way of other boats as possible. Although the creek is heavily used by both fishing and pleasure boats, the environment has a nice ambience, particularly at night.

MILE 278.9 ANCHORAGE

This anchorage is on the opposite side of the river from Joe Wheeler State Park. It's the second embayment upstream from Daymark 278.2. There are two coves but enter only the one at port where the water will be about 20 feet deep at normal pool. Space is limited here so you may need to anchor bow and stern. There are no buildings, the gently sloping banks are wooded, and you will have a good view of the river while being protected from all but northwest winds.

MILE 285.0

Here on the north side of the river is the mouth of Elk River. This river drains a large area of south central Tennessee, and has a marked channel extending for about 15 miles upstream. After about five miles, the river is crossed by the U.S. 72 bridge which has a vertical clearance of 28.0 feet at normal pool. Water depth in the channel will be at least 10 feet at normal pool but watch for snags and be careful if you venture outside the channel.

MILE 285.1 ANCHORAGE

On the opposite side of the river from the mouth of Elk River is the Goldfield Branch embayment. Water depth will be about 15 feet at normal pool halfway up the embayment. The gently sloping banks are wooded, there are no structures, and there's enough space for you to swing on one anchor. A road, however, crosses the embayment at the far end. This anchorage affords a good view of the lake and will protect you from all but northwest winds.

**MILE 287.0
MARINA
RESTAURANT
LODGING**

Look to the opposite side of the river after passing Daymark 286.2 and you'll see Lucy Branch Resort and Marina.

*Lucy Branch Resort & Marina
6120 Snake Road
Athens, Alabama 35611
256-729-6443
1-800-242-9824*

Open all year, 8AM until 5PM. Can accommodate boats up to 64 feet in covered slips and up to 40 feet in open slips. Has 10 transient slips and 30 amp and 50 amp electrical service. Water depth at dock is 15 feet at normal pool. Has gas and diesel fuel. Has launch ramp, pump out station, some groceries, snacks, limited boating supplies, ice, showers, and laundromat. On premises and available for use by boaters is a swimming pool, tennis, and miniature golf. Monitors channel 16. Accepts MasterCard, and Visa credit cards.

Restaurant: The restaurant at the marina serves light foods, mostly sandwiches, from a limited menu.

Lodging: The marina has 2-bedroom executive and honeymoon cabins along the river bank that can be rented by the day, week, or month.

MILE 288.1

A line of buoys that marks the navigation channel begins here and continues for the next 15 miles.

Also, you will be able to clearly see the distinctive stack that identifies TVA's Browns Ferry nuclear power plant. The stack, part of the plant's cooling system, is 660 feet high. When the first of the plant's three units began operating in 1974, Browns Ferry was the world's largest nuclear power generating plant.

DAYMARK 294.9

Here, the river's width is deceptive. Almost all the water outside the navigation channel is extremely shallow.

MILE 297.5

Just after you pass under this aerial power crossing, the navigation channel splits to pass on each side of Finley Island most of which is submerged. The channels rejoin about two miles farther upstream.

At starboard is the beginning of an industrial complex that stretches for nearly five miles into downtown Decatur, Alabama.

Decatur dates from 1820 when land taken from the Cherokee Indians was sold at auction. The town became important during the Civil War because of the Memphis & Charleston Railroad bridge built across the Tennessee River in 1856.

In 1864, Decatur was almost completely destroyed by Union troops. Within several years, however, wealthy northern industrialists had returned prosperity to the city. Today, Decatur's population is about 53,000.

There are several tourist destinations in Decatur. One is the Old State Bank. Opened in 1833, it's Alabama's oldest bank building and one of the few structures in Decatur to survive the Civil War. Walking tours can be taken through historic districts consisting of

Alabama's largest collection of historically significant Victorian and Craftsman homes.

Point Mallard, a 750-acre city park, features an 18-hole championship golf course and the Nation's first wave pool. Also of interest is Cook's Natural Science Museum with its extensive collection of insects, minerals, and mounted animals and the Wheeler Wildlife Refuge visitor center.

MILE 303.7
FUEL

At starboard immediately upstream from the seven chimneyed condominium is the Brickyard Landing Marina. Although primarily a dry storage facility, the marina also is a convenient refueling stop except for very large boats which may have difficulty maneuvering in the narrow harbor. Favor the upstream side when entering. Water depth at the fuel dock is about eight feet at normal pool.

The marina is open 8AM until 8PM from May 1 to Labor Day, and 10AM until 4PM for the remainder of the year. Also available besides gas are snacks and light foods. Accepts MasterCard, Visa, Discover and American Express credit cards. For more information, call 256-350-1449.

MILE 304.4

This railway bridge is a lift span. In the down position, vertical clearance is 9.8 feet at normal pool. Call the bridge tender on channel 13 or 16 if you need the bridge raised.

This bridge is on the same site as the Memphis & Charleston Railroad bridge burned by the Union Army on April 27, 1862, to stop a Confederate advance.

MILE 305.0
MARINA
RESTAURANT
FOOD

After you leave the railroad bridge behind but before you pass under the highway bridges, you will see downtown Decatur at starboard. At port is Riverwalk Marina which you enter by passing the fuel dock.

Riverwalk Marina
P.O. Box 1865
Decatur, Alabama 35602
256-340-9170

Open all year 8AM until 5PM. Can accommodate boats up to 80 feet. Has eight transient slips and 30 amp and 50 amp electrical service. Water depth at the fuel dock is 12 feet at normal pool. Has gas and diesel fuel. Has launch ramp. Mechanic for gas and diesel engine repairs is on call. Taxi service is available to nearby restaurants, shopping malls and grocery stores. Transportation also is available to Huntsville International Airport which is 12 miles away. Monitors channel 16. Accepts MasterCard, Visa and American Express credit cards.

Restaurant: A seasonal (Memorial Day to Labor Day) outdoor restaurant on the premises serves snacks and light foods.

Food: Steak dinners and pizza are available for delivery to the marina.

Immediately upstream from the marina are the two new bridges that take U.S. highways 31 and 72 across the river. Beyond the bridges is a complex of grain elevators through which considerable grain moves to support north Alabama's poultry industry. These elevators also are used for shipping soybeans, an important crop on many farms in the region.

At port is the beginning of the Wheeler National Wildlife Refuge. It extends along most of both sides of the river for nearly 15 miles.

This refuge of 34,500 acres is valuable to both wildlife and recreation interests but is under increasing pressure because of the area's population and industrial growth.

The refuge is the easternmost national wildlife refuge on the lower Mississippi Flyway and is the southernmost wintering ground of Canada geese. Thousands of geese and ducks overwinter here. The refuge's visitors have included 304 species of birds plus many mammals including deer, fox, beaver, muskrats, and mink.

MILE 309.6

This is the I-65 bridge. I-65 begins in Chicago and links such cities as Indianapolis, Louisville, and Nashville, to the north with Birmingham, Montgomery, and Mobile, to the south.

Construction of the bridge was interrupted for several months so that nesting birds in that part of the Wheeler National Wildlife Refuge through which the bridge passes wouldn't be disturbed.

The next 10 miles provide a fine opportunity for you to relax and enjoy the scenery. Although the landscape is far from awe inspiring, it is soothing by virtue of the wildness you haven't seen for quite a few miles.

MILE 319.0

Half hidden behind the hill is a distant tower that's part of the Redstone Arsenal and Marshall Space Flight Center complex. It was here more than 30 years ago that the effort to launch America's space program began.

MILE 324.0

The mountains you see ahead are south of Huntsville, Alabama. They are part of the southern end of the Cumberland Plateau that begins in eastern Kentucky and extends southwest through eastern Tennessee into northern Alabama.

From about here to Guntersville Lock & Dam, the river is usually busy during summer weekends. The situation is further aggravated by the river's narrowness. So stay alert for other boats, water skiers, and swimmers.

DAYMARK 326.0

This is the midpoint on the Tennessee River. You are now exactly halfway between Paducah and where the river begins just east of Knoxville.

MILE 333.2

These twin spans take U.S. 231 across the river. This is one of eastern Alabama's principal north-south highways. You are now about five miles south of downtown Huntsville.

Once a small and quiet county seat town, Huntsville has grown into a busy and thriving city with a population of more than 180,000. It's Alabama's third largest city. Only Birmingham and Mobile are larger.

Here at Redstone Arsenal and Marshall Space Flight Center is where Wernher Von Braun, the world's foremost rocket engineer, helped lead the United States into the space age. Many companies involved in the technology of the Nation's space program established research and development facilities in Huntsville.

During the last few years, however, business and industry in Huntsville have diversified to make the urban economy even stronger.

By a wide margin, the most popular tourist attraction is the Space & Rocket Center. It's the world's largest space museum and has the Nation's largest and finest collection of NASA rockets and army missiles.

There are dozens of hands-on exhibits, flight simulations, a theater with a 67-foot domed screen, and an extensive outdoor exhibit that includes such hardware as military rockets, the 354-foot Saturn V moon rocket, a 98-ton full size model of the Space Shuttle, the only full-scale model of the Hubble Space Telescope, a U.S. Air Force SR-71 Blackbird spy plane, and many artifacts from the Mercury and Apollo space missions.

Also at the Center is the U.S. Space Camp for youth who wish to explore the wonders of aviation and space. Nearly 200,000 trainees from all 50 states and many foreign countries have attended this camp.

Monte Sano State Park is on top of a mountain at the east edge of Huntsville. It covers more than 2,000 acres and offers fine views of the city below. Also on the mountain is Burritt Museum. It's built in the shape of a Maltese cross and contains many exhibits related to Huntsville's history.

Big Spring Park in downtown Huntsville is where John Hunt founded the city in 1805. The park plus the Museum of Art and the Old Town Historic District are popular with tourists.

MILE 333.3
MARINA
FOOD

At port immediately beyond the U.S. 231 bridge is Ditto Landing Marina. It's operated by the City of Huntsville and Madison County. A sign identifies the marina. The entrance is narrow so take your time and enter slowly, especially during summer weekends when boat traffic is usually heavy. Ditto Landing was named for James Ditto, a pioneer who began operating a ferry here in 1807 to help settlers moving into the area. Later, James White from Virginia established a port which became the town of Whitesburg. It was an important cotton shipping center until the coming of the railroads. The Whitesburg post office closed in 1905.

Ditto Landing Marina
P.O. Box 14250, 293 Ditto Landing Road
Huntsville, Alabama 35815
256-883-9420

Open all year, 8AM until 10PM. Can accommodate boats up to 65 feet. Has minimum of four transient slips but "we have never turned anyone away." Has 30 amp and 50 amp electrical service. Water depth at the fuel dock is 10 feet at normal pool. Has gas and diesel fuel. Has launch ramp, ice, showers, laundromat, pump out station, and a few boating supplies. Taxi service to downtown Huntsville is available. Monitors channel 16. Accepts MasterCard, Visa, Discover, and American Express credit cards.

Food: There are no restaurants near the marina. But two fast food establishments will deliver. For pizza, call Terry's Pizza at 881-5987. For steak meals, call Steak-Out at 883-1987.

MILE 336.0

The scenery continues to be more interesting as you look ahead and see Cedar Mountain at starboard.

DAYMARK 339.1
ANCHORAGE

Across from this Daymark is the mouth of the Flint River. This is the best place in the 16 miles between Ditto Landing and Guntersville Dam to anchor off the main river. The Flint appears to be a large stream rather than a river and its narrowness and overgrown banks may tend to discourage you from entering. But water depth will be at least 15 feet at normal pool. There is usually only a slight current.

Stay in the center of the river and go past the abandoned dock to an island which you can see as soon as you enter the river. If you move to starboard out of the main channel, the water depth will be about 10 feet. Except for perhaps an occasional fishing boat, you should have plenty of peace and solitude here as well as excellent wind protection from all directions.

If you choose to anchor in the Flint, leave the Tennessee's navigation channel between the second and third green buoys. When you return to the Tennessee, however, you can turn to port as soon as you leave the Flint and rejoin the navigation channel a short distance upstream.

MILE 344.8

Painted Bluff at port, one of the highest bluffs on the river between here and Paducah, gets its name from the yellow and brown rock.

The buoys just ahead mark the navigation channel that skirts the north side of the river as you approach Guntersville Lock & Dam.

MILE 349.0

Of all the dams on the Tennessee, Guntersville Dam may be the least visually obtrusive. Wedged between two hills, the dam is 94 feet high and 3,979 feet long. Construction began in 1935 and was completed in 1939.

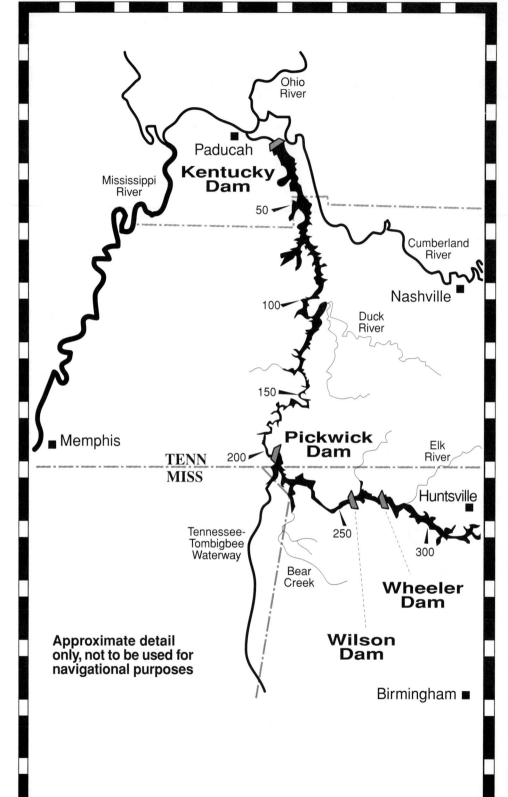

The Tennessee River

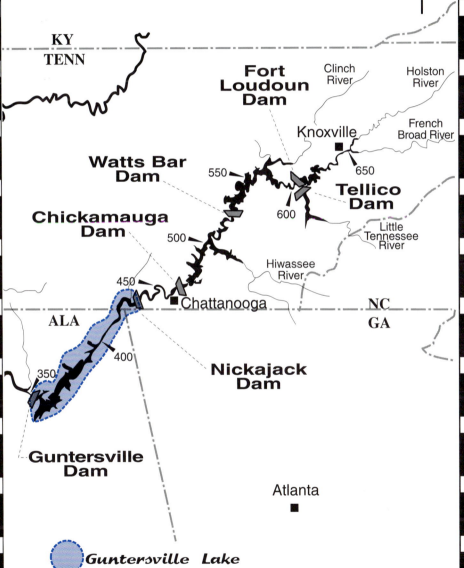

N

KY
TENN

Fort Loudoun Dam

Clinch River

Holston River

Knoxville

French Broad River

Watts Bar Dam

550

650

Tellico Dam

600

Chickamauga Dam

500

Little Tennessee River

450

Hiwassee River

Chattanooga

NC
GA

ALA

400

Nickajack Dam

350

Guntersville Dam

Atlanta

Guntersville Lake

Nothing you have yet seen on the Tennessee prepares you for the view as you leave Guntersville Lock. Said one boater, "My gosh, it looks just like a park."

Indeed, it does. The expanse of water between cliffs and forested hills rising to 600 feet above the lake invite you to look, admire, and explore.

In prehistoric times, the Tennessee didn't flow here. Instead, it continued southwestward from what is now Chattanooga and Guntersville toward central Alabama. But a massive uplift forced the river to change course. So it gnawed its way through the southern end of the Cumberland plateau where you are now and continued westward across northern Alabama.

Guntersville Lake is often more than two miles wide. With an area of 67,900 acres and a length of 76 miles, it's the second largest lake in the Tennessee River system. Only Kentucky Lake is larger.

Hydrilla and water milfoil, the two aquatic plants mentioned under Daymark 25.4, are widespread in Guntersville Lake. Many embayments have become so infested that they are now useless to boaters.

For this reason, be careful when you venture off the navigation channel. Because these weeds can grow in water up to about 20 feet deep, you are likely to encounter them before you reach the floating masses of vegetation. Also keep in mind that they will often give you false depthfinder readings.

DAYMARK 349.5
ANCHORAGE

For the first time in many miles, you now have a choice of anchorages.

This Daymark at port and the two mooring cells mark the entrance to the first one. This embayment is indicated on the official charts as a First Class harbor so make sure you anchor beyond the white cross markers where water depth will be about 15 feet at normal pool. The wooded banks range from moderately steep to very steep and there are no structures. You will be protected from all but south winds, have plenty of space to swing on one anchor, and have a good view of the lake.

MILE 350.1

About midway between the first anchorage mentioned above and Daymark 350.4, look for a cave just above the waterline. The cave's entrance is protected by a wire fence. This is a sanctuary for the endangered Gray bat. At dusk, thousands of bats fly from the cave to feed on insects.

**MILE 351.5
ANCHORAGE**

This is the entrance to Honeycomb Creek. At starboard as you enter is Goat Island, so named because a farmer kept a herd of goats there before the Civil War.

On the back or north side of the island is a shallow cove with a water depth of about 20 feet at normal pool. There's plenty of space here to swing on one anchor and the view across open water to the mountains beyond is magnificent. During the summer and especially on weekends, however, boating activity is heavy in this area, mostly because farther up the embayment are a campground and launch ramp.

MILE 352.2

Look carefully about 300 feet past the channel at the upstream end of Goat Island and about halfway up the side of the cliff. There, carved in stone, is the following inscription: "Gen. Andrew Jackson 1813-1914, Ala. D.A.R." The inscription dates back to 1914 and is over a cave, now underwater, where supplies were stored for General Jackson while he was enroute to the Creek Indian War.

For the next three miles, the river curves gently to starboard and gradually becomes much wider. Eventually, you will see the twin spans of the George S. Houston bridge, U.S. 431. This is an important highway link between Huntsville to the northwest and Gadsden and Anniston to the south.

At the south end of the bridge is the site of an Indian-pioneer village. "Head-man" of the village was John Gunter, a full-blooded Scotsman who came to live among the Indians in 1785.

Guntersville, named after Gunter and built on a peninsula, has a population of about 8,000. It has always been an important river port, particularly during the Civil War. Today, grain for much of the poultry production in northeast Alabama passes through terminals that dot the edges of Guntersville's harbor.

In recent years, Guntersville has become increasingly popular as a tourist destination. Also, more retirees who appreciate the water, moderate climate, and relaxed pace, are moving to the area. Many boaters from such nearby cities as Birmingham keep boats here.

MILE 357.4
MARINA
RESTAURANT

To port and before you reach the bridge is a marked channel leading to Alred Marina about two miles away. You will be able to see the marina from the main channel. Also, there's a small sign on the island where you make the turn. The fuel pumps are on the end of the third dock.

Alred Marina
351 Marina Road
Guntersville, Alabama 35976
256-582-4400

Open all year, 7AM until 6PM Monday through Saturday, 8AM until 5PM on Sunday, April through October, and 7AM until 4PM Monday through Friday, 8AM until 4PM on Saturday and 9AM until 3PM on Sunday for the remainder of the year. Can accommodate boats up to 70 feet. Has six transient slips and 30 amp and 50 amp electrical service. Water depth at the fuel dock is 10 feet at normal pool. Has gas and diesel fuel which are available 24 hours a day with a credit card pay-at-pump system. Has launch ramp. Complete service facilities include parts department, 30-ton travel lift and marine railway for up to 60-foot boats. Can do wood work, welding, painting, and fiberglass repair. Ship's store has good selection of boating supplies plus snacks and convenience store grocery items. Has ice, showers and laundromat. Arrangements can be made for use of courtesy vehicle or rental cars.

Restaurant: On weekends during the summer months, a restaurant on the premises serves sandwiches and short orders.

MILE 358.1
MARINA

Just after you pass under the bridge, turn sharply to starboard and cruise parallel to the bridge to reach Guntersville Marina. The fuel dock is just inside the breakwater.

Guntersville Marina
201 Blount Avenue
Guntersville, Alabama 35976
256-582-6867

Open all year, 7AM until 7PM. Can accommodate boats up to 80 feet. The number of transient slips varies. Has 30 amp and 50 amp electrical service. Water depth at the fuel dock is 15 feet at normal pool. Has gas and diesel fuel. Has ice and limited boating supplies including maps, charts, and cruising guides. In downtown Guntersville, which begins two blocks from the marina, are banks, the post office, a supermarket, and many other services and retail stores. Marina operator will provide transportation in her car. Monitors channel 16. Accepts MasterCard and Visa credit cards.

MILE 358.5
MARINA

Directly across the lake from Guntersville Marina is Signal Point Marina. You'll recognize it by the large blue building that's the marina's dry boat storage facility. As you near the marina, head for the fuel dock which is directly in front of the dry storage building. The small white buoys in front of the slips at starboard mark a small area of very shallow water.

Signal Point Marina
100 Marina Lane
Guntersville, Alabama 35976
256-582-3625

Open all year, 8AM until dusk. Can accommodate boats up to 70 feet. Transients are welcome. Water depth at the fuel dock is eight feet at normal pool. Has 30 amp and 50 amp electrical service. Has gas and diesel fuel. Has ice, showers, snacks, and 24-hour security. Downtown Guntersville is about three miles away. Courtesy car is available for travel to the Boaz Outlet Center, one of the Nation's largest, which is 15 miles away. "Whatever your needs, we will do all we can to supply them." Monitors channel 16. Accepts MasterCard, Visa, Discover, and American Express credit cards.

MILE 361.0
ANCHORAGE

As you continue upriver, you'll see the large Short Creek embayment on your starboard side. Water depth will range from 15 to 20 feet at normal pool for about two-thirds of its length. There's plenty of space for swinging on one anchor and you will have a wide choice of anchoring locations. Wind protection will depend on where you anchor. This is, however, a busy place on summer weekends. The highway at the end of the embayment leads to Lake Guntersville State Park.

MILE 361.7
ANCHORAGE

If Short Creek isn't to your liking, then continue upstream three-fourths of a mile to this embayment. About half way into it, water depth will be about 15 feet at normal pool. There's space enough here to swing on one anchor and you will be protected from all but northwest winds. The nearly level to gently sloping banks are wooded on one side and occupied by state park cabins on the other. The cabins, however, are nearly hidden by trees.

If you continue up this side of the river, you will pass the state park dock beyond which is a beach and camping area. The park lodge and restaurant are on top of the mountain. Unfortunately, there is no dock for transient boaters nor does the park provide transportation from the river to the lodge.

Unless you wish to continue past this area to explore Town Creek ahead, rejoin the main navigation channel between Daymark 363.4 and the red buoy immediately downstream from it. Although the water becomes more shallow as you approach the channel, it will be about 10 feet deep at normal pool.

Ahead, the lake widens to almost two miles and the landscape becomes more expansive.

MILE 367.0

The width of Guntersville Lake can be deceiving. For example, a secondary channel here leads up Mill Creek to a boat dock. But most of the creek is choked with hydrilla and water milfoil that will quickly foul your prop. The lesson is clear: Be very careful when you leave the navigation channel!

MILE 369.0

This small embayment is most suitable if you need to get off the main river for a while. Water depth is about nine feet at normal pool at the entrance and for a short distance.

In this vicinity was Coste, an Indian town of the Koosita Tribe visited by Hernando DeSoto's expedition in 1540. The site of the town plus many Indian mounds are now covered with water.

MILE 378.0
MARINA
LODGING
RESTAURANT
ANCHORAGE

Caution! Check your fuel supply before passing Goose Pond Marina identified by a sign at port. The next available fuel is at Hales Bar Marina 53 miles upstream.

To reach the marina, turn to port here and follow the marked channel. Its depth will be about seven feet at normal pool but don't be alarmed if your depthfinder reads somewhat less. Hydrilla and milfoil you will see floating on both sides of the channel is also growing on the bottom and causes many false readings.

Goose Pond Colony is a 360-acre recreation complex owned and operated by the city of Scottsboro, Alabama. It features a marina and an 18 hole, 6,900 yard, par 72 golf course. The pro shop, less than a mile from the marina, has a snack bar, putting green, driving range, and cart rentals. The course has a beautiful setting, is of championship quality, and is visited by golfers from throughout the eastern United States.

Goose Pond Marina
417 Ed Hembree Drive
Scottsboro, Alabama 35768
256-259-3027

Open all year, 7AM until 9PM every day February through September, and 7AM until 6:30PM for remainder of year. Can accommodate boats up to 100 feet. Has four transient slips with 30 amp and 50 amp electrical service. Water depth at fuel dock is 12 feet at normal pool. Has gas and diesel fuel. Has ice, snacks, limited boat supplies, pump out station, and facilities for repairing gas engines. Monitors channel 16. Accepts MasterCard, Visa, and American Express credit cards.

Lodging: Goose Pond Colony has several ranch style and A-frame vacation cottages that can be rented by the night or week. All have a dock on the water and are within 300 yards of the golf course pro shop. These cottages are very popular so reservations are a must. Call 256-259-2884 or 1-800-268-2884 for more information.

Restaurant: Crawdaddy's Two on the premises serves seafood and steaks. The restaurant is on the water and is accessible by a "T" pier where water depth is about five feet at normal pool. Open Wednesday through Saturday. For more information call 256-574-3071.

Anchorage: The large circular embayment bordered by the marina and the golf course offers a water depth of about 10 feet at normal pool. It certainly isn't secluded but because this is an enforced no-wake area,

115

you're not likely to be bothered by wakes from other boats. This water is fairly open so you will be exposed to some wind from every direction. There's plenty of space on which to swing on one anchor and the scenery is easy to take.

MILE 379.0
ANCHORAGE

If there's too much activity at Goose Pond Marina for you, then this anchorage just a mile farther upstream will be much more to your liking. It's indicated on the official charts as a Second Class harbor and has three sets of pilings down the middle. Water depth as you enter will be about 12 feet at normal pool. Hydrilla and water milfoil growing on the bottom, however, may give you false readings. Don't tie up to the pilings. Instead, anchor between the last set of pilings and the bank at port where water depth will be about 10 feet. There's plenty of space on which to swing on one anchor, the nearly flat to moderately steep banks are completely wooded, there are no structures, and you will have good wind protection except from the west. Another bonus is that you will have a fine view of Sand Mountain on the other side of the river.

MILE 380.0

You should now be able to see the old and new spans of the Comer Bridge which take Alabama 35 & 40 across the river. These highways link Huntsville and Scottsboro with the top of Sand Mountain and I-59 which connects Chattanooga with Birmingham.

After you pass under the bridge, low tree covered islands clearly reveal where the banks of the river were before Guntersville Dam was built.

MILE 388.0
ANCHORAGE

At starboard is the buoyed entrance to Jones Creek, a favorite anchorage for local boaters.

Entrance depth at normal pool will be about 10 feet but becomes slightly greater once you are well inside. Although the green buoys appear to be too close to the bank, water depth holds true. Carefully follow the well marked channel until you pass the last green buoy. If you wish to go no farther, you can turn to port here and continue for a short distance before dropping anchor. Because the water here is more than a half mile wide, you will have virtually no wind protection. But if the weather is good, the tradeoff is more than worth it. Except for a distant Boy Scout camp to the south and occasional fishermen, there's nothing to disturb the sweeping vista of wide water and distant mountains.

DAYMARK 391.6

Directly across from this Daymark is TVA's Bellefonte nuclear power plant. Construction began in 1974 but the plant was never completed. Now in deferred status, it's unlikely the plant will ever become operational. The cooling towers are 587 feet high.

DAYMARK 392.1

Here, the navigation channel swings to starboard around Bellefonte Island and to the base of Sand Mountain.

This mountain, which has been on your starboard side since you left Guntersville, is one of Alabama's most prominent land features. It's more than 50 miles long and about 15 miles wide. The fertile soil on top of the mountain is a sandy loam ideal for many crops including potatoes and other vegetables. Until a few years ago, the mountain reportedly had the highest concentration of small farms in the United States.

MILE 394.3

About a half mile beyond the upstream end of Bellefonte Island is the entrance to Mud Creek. If you must get off the river in an emergency and the length of your boat is about 40 feet or less, you can do it here. Go slow because the creek is narrow and there are snags along both banks. Water depth will be about 15 feet at normal pool for a short distance after you leave the river but becomes considerably less when the creek broadens.

MILE 399.0

The mountains are now behind you and the view ahead reveals a broader and flatter landscape. Visible above Crow Creek Island is the stack at TVA's Widow's Creek power plant. The stack, 1,000 feet high, is one of the tallest structures in the Tennessee Valley region.

MILE 400.5

The navigation channel is on the starboard side of Crow Creek Island which is a waterfowl wildlife refuge. About midway upstream on the port side, however, is the entrance to Crow Creek. As with Mud Creek at Mile 394.3, consider Crow Creek as an option if you must get off the river in an emergency. For the first few hundred feet, the creek is narrow. Water depth, however, will be about 15 feet at normal pool but becomes considerably more shallow when the creek broadens about a quarter of a mile upstream.

MILE 403.1

This is the Captain John Snodgrass bridge and Alabama 117, a highway linking several small communities with U.S. 72 to the west and I-59 to the east.

MILE 407.5

At port is the Widows Creek power plant, the third largest of TVA's 12 coal-fired plants.

MILE 410.0

Emptying into the Tennessee here is Long Island Creek. It's too narrow to be a good anchorage. Also, a bridge with about nine feet of vertical clearance at normal pool crosses the creek only a few hundred feet from the main river. But it can be used in an emergency or if weather threatens. Water depth ranges from about 15 feet to 20 feet at normal pool upstream as far as the bridge. A strong south or southwest wind could make entering and maneuvering tricky.

MILE 414.4

This railway bridge is a lift span. In the down position, vertical clearance is 34.2 feet at normal pool. Call the bridge tender on channel 13 or 16 if you need the bridge raised.

MILE 416.3

As you pass under the aerial power crossing, you will be leaving Alabama and entering Tennessee.

DAYMARK 416.9

Here at the upstream end of Bridgeport Island, you will have a wide view of the Cumberland Plateau. The top is more than 1,100 feet above the river.

MILE 418.5

The South Pittsburg highway bridge, Tennessee 156, is one of the newer bridges across the river and one of the most architecturally interesting. It features the suspended arch type of construction. Other designs require considerably more heavy steel in the approaches. Also, because the roadway is supported from above, the bridge can be built lower relative to the river banks while maintaining plenty of vertical clearance.

Another distinctive feature of this bridge is that navigational horizontal clearance is 730 feet, the widest of any bridge on the Tennessee.

MILE 420.3

You are now at the southern end of Sequatchie Valley. From here you can see both sides of it. This is one of the world's two rift valleys. The other is the Great Victoria Valley in Africa. Both were created by the earth's surface literally splitting apart. Sequatchie Valley is more than 125 miles long but never more than five miles wide. Because the cliffs provide ideal conditions for hang gliding enthusiasts, the valley is known as the "Hang Gliding Capital of the East."

The valley is drained by the Sequatchie River which joins the Tennessee about three miles farther upstream.

MILE 424.7

This is Nickajack Dam which replaced the Hales Bar Dam formerly located six miles upstream. It's 81 feet high and 3,767 feet long and is the newest dam on the river. Construction began in 1964 and was completed in 1967.

You will notice that the lock is almost in the center of the dam. Space was left between the lock and north end of the dam so another lock could be added if needed.

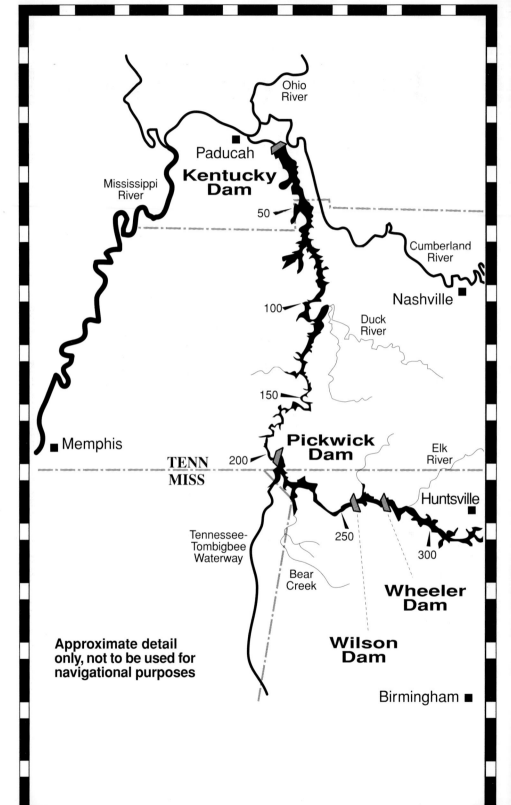

Ohio River

Paducah

Kentucky Dam

Mississippi River

50

Cumberland River

Nashville

100

Duck River

150

Pickwick Dam

200

Memphis

TENN
MISS

Elk River

Huntsville

250

300

Tennessee-Tombigbee Waterway

Bear Creek

Wheeler Dam

Wilson Dam

**Approximate detail
only, not to be used for
navigational purposes**

Birmingham

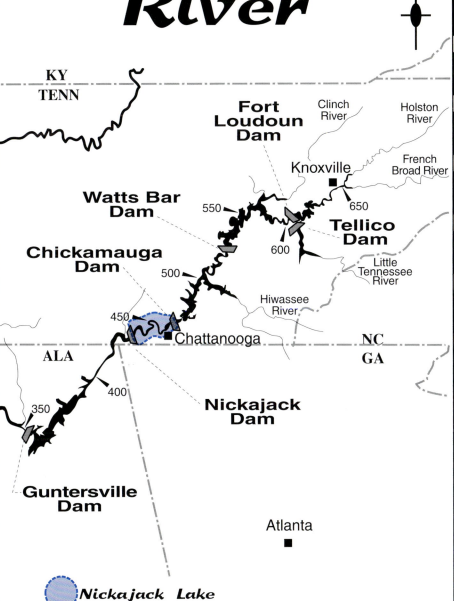

The
Tennessee
River

N

KY
TENN

**Fort
Loudoun
Dam**

Clinch
River

Holston
River

Knoxville

French
Broad River

**Watts Bar
Dam**

550

650

**Tellico
Dam**

600

**Chickamauga
Dam**

500

Little
Tennessee
River

450

Hiwassee
River

Chattanooga

NC
GA

ALA

400

**Nickajack
Dam**

350

**Guntersville
Dam**

Atlanta

Nickajack Lake

Nickajack Lake, 46 miles long, is the second shortest in the Tennessee River system and has little wide water. Yet, it offers memorable features not found on any of the other lakes including water depths of more than 130 feet.

MILE 425.5 ANCHORAGE

The embayment on your port side is part of the Shellmound Recreation Area, site of the annual Fall Color Cruise & Folk Festival held the last two weekends in October. The increasingly popular event features a wide range of activities staged against a backdrop of spectacular fall color.

This is a fine place to pause after you lock through, to anchor while you eat or take a swim, or to anchor overnight. Also, because there really aren't any other good anchorages on Nickajack Lake, you should consider this your only chance to anchor out overnight before continuing upstream to Chattanooga.

The water behind the two mooring cells ranges from about 15 to 20 feet at normal pool. Be extremely cautious, however, if you proceed into upper reaches of this embayment. Stay clear of the area in front of and just beyond the swimming area to avoid water that becomes shallow very quickly. Wakes from boats on the river and from those using the nearby launch ramp may bother you. Also, you will be exposed to southwest winds.

MILE 426.0

From here, you can see the I-24 bridge. This highway begins in southern Illinois and ends in Chattanooga and serves as an important link between the Midwest and Nashville, Chattanooga, and points south.

After you pass Daymark 426.9 at port, you will tend to visually center your attention on the bridge. The channel, however, veers to starboard.

MILE 429.7

This is the Marion County Memorial bridge. Before I-24 was built, U.S.41 was the main highway between Nashville and Chattanooga.

In the distance and ahead of you is the old Hales Bar hydroelectric plant, one of the most historic structures on the Tennessee.

In 1904, Congressman John Moon introduced legislation to build a dam that would generate hydroelectric power and improve upstream navigation. The bill passed and the Chattanooga & Tennessee River Power Company soon began construction.

For the next eight years, the 5,000 workers involved with the project faced considerable risk. Construction accidents resulted in many injuries and several deaths. Also, there were bloody labor troubles. Finally, in November, 1913, the Hales Bar Hydro Plant was completed. It was the world's second largest hydroelectric generating plant. Only Niagara was larger.

The plant was dedicated with what may have been the greatest celebration in Chattanooga's history. Bands played, people danced, there were banquets and speeches, and fireworks lit the sky.

But almost from the beginning, there was a serious problem of water leaking through rock strata under the dam. Faced with exorbitant costs for uncertain cures to the problem and a navigation lock too small to meet modern navigation needs, TVA decided to remove the dam and replace it with Nickajack Dam.

Today, the old Hales Bar power house, stripped of its machinery, is eerily silent after being the reason for so much jubilation so many years ago.

MILE 431.2
MARINA
LODGING

Adjoining the Hales Bar power house is the Hales Bar Marina. Check your fuel supply because this is your last chance to refuel for another 40 miles.

There are two ways to reach the marina. One is to turn slightly to starboard just after you pass under the U.S. 41 bridge and go behind the rock piles, mooring cells, and barges usually moored there. As you leave the navigation channel, the water depth will decrease to about 10 feet at normal pool then deepen slightly as you continue upstream. This area is used by commercial shipping companies for storing barges and making up tows. You will see the marina straight ahead. This is the preferred way for boats with a draft of more than about five feet to reach the marina.

The other way is to continue upstream in the navigation channel until you are even with the marina, then turn sharply to starboard. To avoid rocks and shallow water, make sure you don't turn until you are directly across from the fuel dock. Although hydrilla and water milfoil may give you false depthfinder readings, water depth will be about eight feet at normal pool.

Hales Bar Marina
P.O. Box 247, 1265 Hales Bar Road
Guild, Tennessee 37340
423-942-4040

Open all year, 8AM until 5PM (Central Time). Can accommodate boats up to 125 feet. Has 16 transient slips and 30 and 50 amp electrical service. Water depth at the fuel dock is 11 feet at normal pool. Has gas and diesel fuel. Has launch ramp. Can provide repair on gas outboard and I/O units and has diesel mechanic on call. Has ice, snacks, boating supplies, and basic groceries. Has showers on premises about one-fourth mile from the transient slips. Monitors channel 16. Accepts MasterCard, Visa, and Discover credit cards.

Lodging: Both the Chattanooga Choo Choo Hotel in downtown Chattanooga and the Acuff Country Inn about four miles away at the junction of Tennessee 27 and I-24 will send courtesy cars to the marina for anyone wishing accommodations.

Caution! When leaving the marina, be particularly alert for fast moving fishing boats coming downstream and close to the end of the old Hales Bar power house. This blind corner has resulted in many near misses.

DAYMARK 432.4

The stretch of river from here to Chattanooga is known as the "Grand Canyon of the Tennessee." While that may be a bit exaggerated, everyone agrees that the next few miles offer some of the most stunning scenery to be found anywhere on the river. At first, homes and small farms line much of the river bank. But as you leave them behind, the mountains drop steeply into the river which in places is barely 700 feet wide. Also, the river makes a dozen turns during the next 32 miles as it twists through the mountains.

Much of what you will be passing through is part of the Prentice Cooper State Forest and Wildlife Management Area. The slopes are rich with foliage. More than 300 kinds of trees and 900 varieties of wildflowers grow in the Chattanooga area. In fact, nowhere in the world except in central China is there such a wide range of plant life.

MILE 444.6

Here at starboard and 1,100 feet above you is TVA's Raccoon Mountain pumped storage project. A 520-acre lake was created on top of the mountain into which water is pumped from the river during times of slack power use. Then when there are peak demands for electric power, water is allowed to flow down the mountain through giant tubes and turbines to generate electricity.

DAYMARK 445.8

As you approach and pass this Daymark, don't be surprised if your depthfinder shows water as deep as 135 feet. One reason for this extreme depth is that the river follows an ancient earthquake fault.

For the next few miles, the gorge that the Tennessee has carved over millions of years is at its scenic best.

This part of the river is known as "The Pan." Before Hales Bar Dam was built, there were many accidents here. Boats became uncontrollable because of unusual and unpredictable currents. Names given to other troublesome stretches upstream include the "The Skillet," "The Pot," and "The Suck." These names were chosen by early boatmen who thought the boiling and swirling water reminded them of food being cooked.

DAYMARK 451.8

You are now entering the Eastern Time Zone. Set your watch ahead one hour.

Also, you now have a clear view of Signal Mountain, one of Chattanooga's most famous natural landmarks.

MILE 454.5

On the mountain slope at port is a large planting of Kudzu. Native to China and Japan, it was first brought to the United States in 1895 and used as a climbing vine for porches and trellises. Later, it was widely adopted in the

South to help prevent soil erosion. Kudzu has a thick network of roots and enriches the soil through nitrogen-fixing bacteria on its roots. But the vine is very aggressive and can smother trees and cover entire buildings in only one growing season.

DAYMARK 454.6

This Daymark marks the lower end of Williams Island. The island, site of an Indian village and named for a pioneer who lived there, may have served as a French trading post. It also played a brief part in Chattanooga's more recent history.

In April 1862, James J. Andrews, a Union spy, led 21 men through Confederate lines in Marietta, Georgia. There, they captured a railroad engine, the GENERAL, and headed north toward Chattanooga, destroying telegraph communications as they went. Confederate troops in another engine, the TEXAS, gave chase and eventually caught the GENERAL. Andrews was jailed in Chattanooga but escaped and managed to get as far as Williams Island. There, he was recaptured then taken to Atlanta and hanged.

MILE 455.2

The brick buildings on top of the river bank at port just after you pass under the aerial crossing are part of the Baylor School. Founded in 1893 as a private prep school, it later became a military school, and most recently a co-educational private high school. On the 600-acre campus are several imposing buildings including a chapel.

MILE 455.6

Here, Lookout Mountain, one of America's best known landmarks, comes into view. The mountain thrusts upward more than 2,000 feet above the river and extends for nearly 100 miles into Georgia and Alabama. On its slopes was fought the last battle of the

American Revolution. And it was here in November of 1863 that Union and Confederate forces clashed in the "Battle Above The Clouds."

Today, Lookout Mountain is famous for having the Nation's first military park, the world's steepest passenger railway, and the commercial attractions of Ruby Falls and Rock City.

MILE 460.0

Beginning here and for more than a mile, you will be paralleling I-24 which will be only a few hundred feet away. As you leave the curve and head north, downtown Chattanooga will be ahead of you.

Chattanooga's history began in 1815 when Cherokee descendant Chief John Ross established a ferry across the river and built a trading post. Chattanooga was incorporated in 1839 and became an important commercial center. The city's strategic location and metal industries were the main reasons the Confederates tried desperately to retain control during the Civil War.

Today, Chattanooga has a population of about 175,000 and is important as a manufacturing, wholesale, and retail center. It also draws many tourists traveling between the Midwest and Florida.

There is so much to see and do in Chattanooga that many transient boaters rent a car and spend several days here. Besides Lookout Mountain there is the historic and beautifully restored Terminal Station which when completed in 1909 had the largest brick arch in the world. There's also the 8,000-acre Chickamauga-Chattanooga National Military Park which is the Nation's oldest and largest.

The latest attraction is the Tennessee Aquarium on the river waterfront. This $45 million freshwater life center is home to more than 7,000 animals, including 300 species of fish, reptiles, amphibians, birds, and mammals. The aquarium is housed on four levels all of which have impressive exhibits. One tank, the largest freshwater tank in the world, holds 138,000 gallons. From the top of the building you will have a wide view of the Tennessee River in which live more species of fish than in any other river in North America.

Chattanooga serves as a hub for many outdoor activities including rafting on nearby Ocoee River and Hiwassee River.

MILE 463.6

Just ahead is the Olgiatti Bridge which takes I-124 and U.S. 27 across the river. At starboard is Ross's Landing Marina. Although it has been inoperative for several years, plans are being made to reopen it. For the latest information on the status of this marina call the Chattanooga Parks & Recreation Department at 423-757-7529.

MILE 464.1

This is the Chief John Ross drawbridge. Immediately before you pass under the bridge you'll see the architecturally distinctive Tennessee Aquarium. A dock has been built for visiting pleasure boaters. No overnight docking is allowed and the city assumes no responsibility for the safety of your boat. The amount of current here depends on how much water is being released through Chickamauga Dam seven miles upstream. So make sure your boat is well secured.

MILE 464.2

This is the historic Walnut Street Bridge which dates back more than 100 years. After being closed to traffic a few years ago, it was scheduled to be demolished. But Chattanooga citizens rallied and saved the structure. The bridge now has the distinction of being the world's longest pedestrian walkway over water.

MILE 464.5

This is the Veteran's Memorial Bridge. It crosses Maclellan Island which is an Audubon Wildlife Refuge.

MILE 468.2

At starboard is the mouth of South Chickamauga Creek. It drains much of the east side of Chattanooga.

MILE 471.0

Soon after you pass under the C.B. Robinson highway bridge you will arrive at Chickamauga Dam. With a height of 129 feet, it's the second highest dam on the Tennessee River. The dam is 5,800 feet long. Construction began in 1936 and was completed in 1940.

It received its name from a warlike tribe that separated from the main body of the Cherokee Indians. The tribe lived in a series of villages that extended nearly a mile along Chickamauga Creek.

Because of the great number of pleasure boats in the Chattanooga area, this lock has more traffic than any other lock on the Tennessee.

Most of the other locks on the Tennessee empty to the side but this one empties in front of the gate. Also, there are only four floating mooring posts, two opposite each other at each end of the lock. If several other boats are locking through, you may be asked to tie up to another boat. So be ready with extra fenders.

As you approach the lock, you will pass under the Southern Railway bridge. Above the lock is the Wilkes T. Thrasher bridge and Tennessee 153 which is a heavily traveled highway linking Chattanooga's northern urban areas.

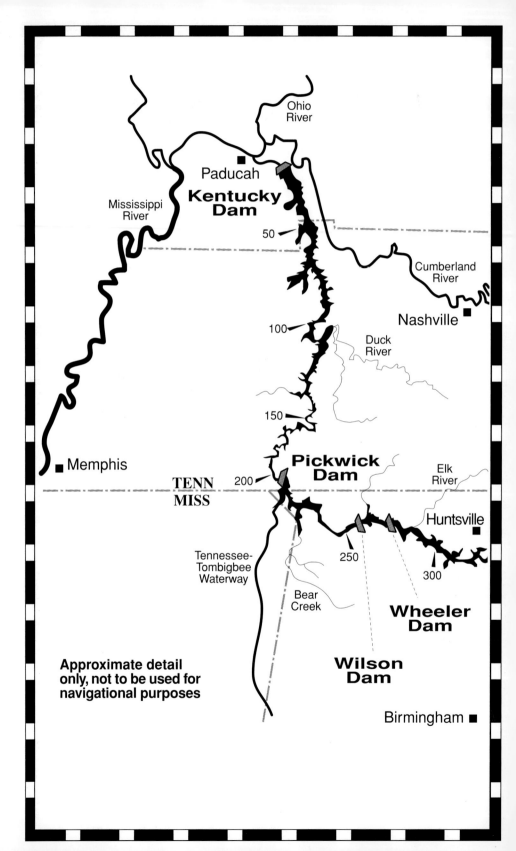

The Tennessee River

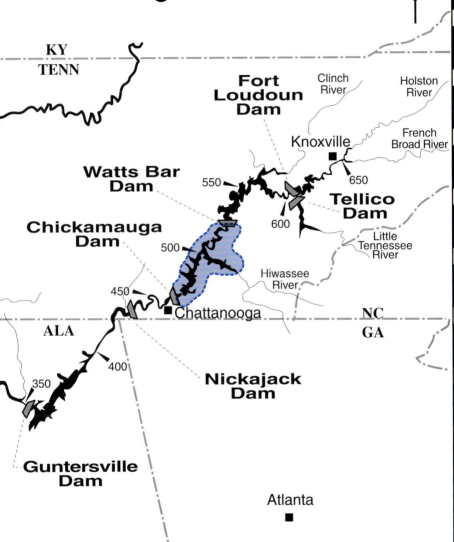

N

KY
TENN

Fort
Loudoun
Dam

Clinch
River

Holston
River

Knoxville

French
Broad River

Watts Bar
Dam

550

650

Tellico
Dam

Chickamauga
Dam

600

Little
Tennessee
River

500

450

Hiwassee
River

Chattanooga

NC
GA

ALA

400

Nickajack
Dam

350

Guntersville
Dam

Atlanta

Chickamauga Lake

This lake is a water playground not only for local boaters but also those from towns and cities as far away as Atlanta. As a result, the lower end of the lake can be extremely busy on summer weekends.

**MILE 471.4
MARINA**

After you clear the lock, look to starboard to the other side of the lake. In the first embayment upstream from a recreation area is Chickamauga Marina.

*Chickamauga Marina
3001 Kings Point Road
Chattanooga, Tennessee 37416
423-622-0821*

Open all year, 8:30AM until 7:30PM, April 1 to after Labor Day, then 8:30AM until 5:30PM for remainder of the year. Can accommodate boats to 60 feet. Has at least 6 transient slips. Has 30 amp and 50 amp electrical service. Water depth at the fuel dock is 12 feet at normal pool. Has gas and diesel fuel. Has full service department including repair of gas and diesel engines. Has hydraulic trailer for haulouts.. Has pump out, snacks, ice, a few boating supplies, and showers. Monitors channel 16. Accepts MasterCard, Visa, Discover, and American Express credit cards.

**MILE 471.7
MARINA**

Almost directly across the lake from Chickamauga Marina is Lake Shore Marina. It's most easily identified by the apartment complex on a bluff upstream from the marina.

*Lake Shore Marina
5600 Lake Resort Terrace
Chattanooga, Tennessee 37415
423-870-2000*

Open all year, 9AM until 5PM and longer on weekends April 15 to after Labor Day. Closed weekends through the winter, then 8:30AM until 5PM the remainder of the year. Can accommodate boats up to 50 feet. Call first for transient dockage. Has 30 amp and 50 amp electrical service. Water depth at the fuel dock is 15 feet at normal pool. Has gas. Has full service repair facilities for gas engines. Has snacks, limited groceries, and a good selection of boating supplies. A much more complete selection of groceries is available at a convenience store one-fourth mile away. Monitors channel 71. Accepts MasterCard, Visa, and Discover credit cards.

MILE 475.8
ANCHORAGE

This is Nance Hollow, the first of two anchorages closest to Chickamauga Dam. Water depth will be about 20 feet at normal pool then tapers to about eight feet up to near the launch ramp. The wooded banks in this narrow and secluded embayment are moderately steep and there are no structures nearby. But wakes from boats using the launch ramp and from boats in the main river may bother you. You will be protected from all wind and can probably swing on one anchor. Residential development is occurring in this area so this anchorage may not be secluded for much longer.

MILE 476.2
ANCHORAGE

This embayment, somewhat more open than the one at Mile 475.8, is just beyond the rock wall known as Grays Bluff. The water here will be about 12 feet deep at normal pool for about two-thirds of its length. There are no structures on the moderately steep to very steep banks. You can easily swing on one anchor here and although you will be exposed to southern winds, the view is scenic.

DAYMARK 476.5

Here, the river makes a sharp turn to starboard. After another mile you will see Harrison Bay. **137**

At first, it will be ahead of you then will be at starboard as the river turns to the north.

**MILE 477.5
MARINA
RESTAURANT
LODGING**

A secondary channel leads off to starboard here, follows the perimeter of Harrison Bay, then rejoins the navigation channel at Daymark 478.4.

After about a mile on the secondary channel, you will see a large embayment at starboard. At the end of it and clearly visible is the private Chattanooga Yacht Club.

A half mile farther you will see Island Cove Marina & Resort also at starboard.

*Island Cove Marina & Resort
6701 Highway 58, P.O. Box 489
Harrison, Tennessee 37341
423-344-8331*

Open all year, 8AM until 6PM Monday through Saturday and 9AM until 6PM on Sunday from early April until late October, and closes at 5PM every day for the remainder of the year. Can accommodate boats up to 60 feet. Number of transient slips varies. Has 30 amp and 50 amp electrical service. Water depth at the fuel dock is 12 feet at normal pool. Has launch ramp. Facilities for gas engine repairs include a 40-ton lift. Has ice, showers, laundromat, snacks, and extensive selection of boating supplies. Swimming pool on premises is available to transient boaters. A one-acre island is available for private parties. Can provide transportation to nearby variety stores and supermarket. Monitors channel 16. Accepts MasterCard, Visa, and American Express credit cards.

Restaurant: The Durty Parrot Pub on the premises is open all year with lunch and dinner being served every day during summer months. Traditional dishes are served from a menu but Caribbean cuisine is the specialty.

Motel: This facility on the premises has twelve large rooms that overlook the marina. Reservations are necessary.

Upon leaving the marina you may want to retrace your route in returning to the main river.

Your other choice is to continue to follow the marked channel around Harrison Bay in which case the information shown below under Daymark 478.4 will be in reverse. If you do, note from the official charts that at Island Cove Marina & Resort the green buoys at port change to red. Also, you'll be paralleling Tennessee 58 for a short distance. This busy highway skirts the east side of the river for more than 60 miles.

DAYMARK 478.4
FUEL
ANCHORAGES

Caution! If you bypassed the secondary channel back at Mile 477.5 but wish to enter it here, don't turn to starboard off the main channel until you can properly enter the marked secondary channel. Extremely shallow water in this area is described by one local boater as "a real outdrive graveyard." After about a half mile you will see a marked channel at port leading to the dock at Harrison Bay State Park.

Gas is available from 8AM until 8PM daily throughout the year. You may anchor overnight near the dock but no overnight docking is allowed. For more information, call 423-344-6214.

Anchorages: About a half mile farther up the secondary channel at port is Dog Leg Slough. Soon after you enter the embayment, you will pass the point where a small cove extends off to port. Water depth there will be about 16 feet at normal pool then become about 10 feet a couple of hundred feet beyond. After that, the water quickly becomes much more shallow. You will have a fine view if you anchor close to the point but be more secluded and better protected if you anchor farther up in the cove. In both locations, you will have plenty of space to swing on one anchor. The wooded banks are nearly level, and there are no structures.

About a half mile past Dog Leg Slough, also at port, is an embayment that splits into two coves. The first cove to port is Huss Lowe Slough. The water will be about 10 feet deep at normal pool as you approach the small boat dock which is about two-thirds up the cove at starboard. The wooded banks are nearly level, there are no structures, there's plenty of space to swing on one anchor, and you will be well protected from wind from every direction.

MILE 479.0

From here, you will get your first glimpse of the twin 460-foot cooling towers at TVA's Sequoyah nuclear power plant.

MILE 483.3
ANCHORAGE

Just before you pass under the five aerial power crossings, you will see an embayment at starboard with three pilings. Water depth as you reach the third piling will be about 20 feet at normal pool and only slightly less after you turn to starboard to the best location for anchoring. Along the nearly level banks is a mix of houses, docks, and wooded areas. Wind protection is excellent from every direction except north and there's plenty of space for swinging on one anchor.

MILE 484.0

From here you will have the best view of the Sequoyah nuclear power plant. You may notice some turbulence just after you pass under the aerial crossing. This is caused by reactor cooling water being pumped back into the river at a rate of 1 million gallons per minute.

A maximum temperature rise of five degrees is allowed in the river as a result of releasing the cooling water. When that limit is reached, the cooling towers are used to provide extra cooling. The release of heat is often responsible for dense fog forming in this area.

DAYMARK 487.5
MARINA
RESTAURANT

A marked channel to port begins here and extends up Soddy Creek. Unusually clean water and a landscape of wooded hills makes this one of the most pristine areas of Chickamauga Lake.

Caution! About a half mile up Soddy Creek is a county highway bridge. Vertical clearance at the highest end of the bridge is 17 feet.

After you pass under the bridge, the creek becomes almost a half mile wide and you will be able to see Pine Harbor Marina ahead of you. In terms of the number of boat slips, it's among the largest on the Tennessee River.

Pine Harbor Marina
1145 Poling Circle
Soddy, Tennessee 37379
423-332-3963

Open all year, 9AM until 7PM except closed on Monday and Tuesday. Can accommodate boats up to 50 feet. Has 8 transient slips and 30 amp electrical service. Water depth at the fuel dock is 15 feet at normal pool. Has gas and diesel fuel on a double sided 140-foot fuel dock. Has pump out station. A mechanic is on duty 9AM until 5PM Wednesday through

Sunday. Has ice and snacks. Full grocery service is two miles away and the folks at the marina can arrange transportation. They also can arrange for you to get a rental car. Has a good selection of boating supplies. Monitors channel 16. Accepts MasterCard and Visa credit cards.

Restaurant: Steve's Landing Restaurant overlooks the marina. It's very popular with boaters and the locals because of the excellent food and pleasant atmosphere. The menu is varied but rib dinners are a specialty. The restaurant is closed Monday and Tuesday, open 5AM until 9PM Wednesday and Thursday, 5AM until 10PM Friday, 11:30AM until 10PM on Saturday, and 11:30AM until 9PM on Sunday.

MILE 488.0

Here, the river turns to the northeast and offers an almost straight stretch of wide water for nearly 10 miles.

MILE 494.7
MARINA
ANCHORAGE

Opposite Daymark 494.9 is the entrance to Sale Creek. About a half mile up the creek on your port side is Sale Creek Marina.

Sale Creek Marina
3900 Lee Pike
Soddy Daisy, Tennessee 37379
423-332-6312
423-332-5921 (Fax)

Open all year, 9AM until 6PM. Can accommodate boats up to 50 feet. Has 5 to 10 transient slips and 30 amp electrical service. Water depth at the fuel dock is 20 feet at normal pool. Has gas and diesel fuel. Has launch ramp, 15-ton lift, and can do minor repairs on both gas and diesel engines. Specializes in parts, supplies, and accessories for sailboats. Does work on props and shafts and can pull engines for replacement. Has *ice, snacks, and showers. Accepts MasterCard, Visa, Discover and American Express credit cards.*

Anchorage: The marked channel on Sale Creek continues past Sale Creek Marina for a short distance before widening into a somewhat circular embayment almost a half mile in diameter. On the north bank is a swimming beach that's part of the Sale Creek Recreational Area. To the left of the beach is a highway bridge. There also are a few houses along the nearly level to very steep banks. Water depth is at least 15 feet at normal pool in and near the marked channel and becomes somewhat more shallow as you move to starboard away from the channel. For more protection from south winds, move closer to the south bank at port where the water will be about 18 feet deep. If you prefer an anchorage with wide water, expansive views, and some activity, this one is excellent.

DAYMARK 498.1 ANCHORAGE

To reach this anchorage, turn to port immediately after reaching this Daymark. But use caution and go slow. Water depth immediately after you leave the navigation channel is only about eight feet at normal pool. Beyond this shallow area, water depth increases to about 12 feet at normal pool and holds to that depth until you are about half way up the embayment. The almost flat to moderately steep banks are wooded and there is only one structure. You will have plenty of space on which to swing on one anchor and be well protected from all but southeast winds.

MILE 499.4

This new bridge replaced the Blythe Ferry, one of the last ferries on the Tennessee. Tennessee 60 links the cities of Dayton to the north with Cleveland to the south.

At starboard is one of the two navigatable mouths of the Hiwassee River. The second is about two miles farther upstream. Triangular shaped Hiwassee Island lies between them.

The Hiwassee, one of the Tennessee's largest tributaries, begins almost 100 miles to the east in the mountains of northern Georgia and southwestern North Carolina. Its 2,700-square mile watershed, 95 percent of which is covered with forest and pasture, involves 4,000 miles of streams.

The Hiwassee offers a good opportunity for you to get off the wide water of the Tennessee and take an interesting side trip.

The following entries relate to the Hiwassee River or HR.

CAUTION! If you require a clearance of more than 28 feet at normal pool, you will not be able to pass under the Tennessee 58 highway bridge at HR Mile 7.5. Also, be sure you stay in the navigation channel. Unlike much of the Tennessee, nearly all the water outside the channel is extremely shallow. Finally, there is commercial traffic on the Hiwassee. So keep on the lookout for tows.

HR MILE 2.0

With the twin mouths of the Hiwassee at your stern, you should be able to enjoy peaceful solitude for the next few miles. Both banks of the Hiwassee are part of the Tennessee Wildlife Refuge system.

HR MILE 7.5

This is the Tennessee 58 highway bridge. The highway parallels the Tennessee River and links several small towns between

Chattanooga and Kingston.

HR MILE 7.9
ANCHORAGE

At port is Agency Creek. This is a wide embayment accessible by a narrow channel between the marker and the rock ledge. Expect a water depth of about eight feet as you enter with slightly deeper water inside. Follow the marked channel to the first or second buoy then move to starboard as you look for a place to anchor. Because there are shallow areas throughout this entire embayment, proceed slowly and cautiously. Farther up the channel is a boat dock. Also, homes are scattered along the distant bank. This is open water so you will be exposed to wind from all directions.

HR MILE 12.9
MARINA

At starboard and clearly marked with a sign is the B & B Marina.

B & B Marina
117 Marina Drive
Charleston, Tennessee 37310
615-336-2341

Open all year 9AM until 7PM from April until September every day except closed on Monday and from 10AM until 5PM Thursday through Sunday the remainder of the year. Can accommodate boats up to 60 feet. Has five transient slips and 30 amp and 50 amp electrical power. Water depth at the fuel dock is 11 feet at normal pool. Has gas. Has launch ramp and has full time mechanic on duty who is certified for gas engine repair. Has ice, snacks, and some boating supplies. Monitors channel 16. Accepts Mastercard and Visa credit cards.

HR MILE 15.4

This is the I-75 bridge. Also, this is the beginning of a four-mile stretch with both sides lined with chemical and paper industries and river terminals. Crossing the river at

145

Mile 18.6 is U.S. Highway 11. Before I-75 was built, this was the main highway between Chattanooga and Knoxville.

HR MILE 20.5

This is the end of the navigation channel. Although the water becomes noticeably more shallow, rarely is it less than about 10 feet deep at normal pool.

As the industrial area quickly disappears, you are again greeted with a mix of forest and a few farms and houses. The river banks range from low steep bluffs to level land that when glimpsed through the trees appears to sweep away from the river.

This is usually a quiet environment made even more interesting by the narrowness of the river. But this isn't usually true on weekends when water skiers take advantage of this part of the river to improve their skills.

HR MILE 28.2

Here, as the river curves slightly to port, is Coon Island. This is the generally accepted end of good cruising water on the Hiwassee. Depending on the size of your boat, it may be possible to venture a bit farther. But it isn't advisable because water levels can suddenly fluctuate when water is released or retained by upstream dams.

If you aren't going up the Hiwassee, at least go up the first channel to the junction buoy then turn back on the second channel and rejoin the Tennessee at imposing Garrison Bluff. You will be rewarded with several scenes in which land and water seem to be woven together.

As you pass Daymark 501.9 at the bottom of Garrison Bluff, look to the top of the bluff where you will see a tall wood structure. This is a "hacking station," a medieval term meaning to collect birds out of nests and train them for falconry. This modern version, however, is used to increase the eagle population.

Eaglets about five weeks old are placed in the structure. They are fed without seeing the people who feed them. This prevents the birds from associating humans with food availability. The front doors are opened as soon as the birds are old enough to fly. Because eagles always return to nest where they learned to fly, the hacking station is used to help establish eagle colonies.

DAYMARK 504.4
FUEL

This is the entrance to Richland Creek. Small signs advertise the Blue Water Campground & Boat Dock which is less than a half mile up the creek. The fuel dock is small. But even if you have a large boat, you shouldn't have any trouble docking if you do it slowly and carefully. Although the dock is close to the river bank, water depth at the dock's outer face is about 15 feet at normal pool. Gas and some groceries and snacks are available.

If you don't stop, slow to idle speed as you pass. Boats docked close to the channel could be damaged by your wake.

Scenic Richland Creek is narrow but well marked all the way to where it ends in downtown Dayton, site of the world famous Scopes evolution trial in 1925. The trial, known as "The Monkey Trial," pitted William Jennings Bryan, a candidate for the U.S. presidency in 1896, against Clarence Darrow, America's most famous criminal lawyer.

The Rhea County courthouse where the trial was held was built in 1890 and has been designated an historic landmark and named to the National Register of Historic Places. In the basement is a museum of memorabilia related to the trial. Old photographs, documents, and posters also provide a glimpse of what Dayton was like in its earlier years.

The courthouse is only a short walk from the dock and offers you an excellent opportunity to spend some relaxing time off your boat.

If you take this side trip, go slow, follow the channel markers exactly, and watch your depthfinder. At normal pool, water depth in the channel ranges from 10 to 20 feet for most of the distance.

When you reach the last red buoy in front of the small boat harbor, you have two options. You can tie up at the end of the dock in the small harbor or anchor out and use your dinghy. If you choose to dock, water depth between the channel and the end of the dock will be about six feet at normal pool. Make very sure you make your turn only after you have cleared the last red buoy. Then go no farther than the end of the dock.

The other option is to proceed past the launch ramp ahead of you for a short distance and anchor. Water depth there will range from 10 to 12 feet at normal pool. Beyond the boat dock is a bait shop which you can call at 423-775-2795 if you need more information.

DAYMARK 506.5

For the next several miles, breaks in the trees along the river banks reveal shallow pools rimmed with willows and reeds. These pleasant scenes coupled with the low hills in the distance and a few houses contrast sharply with the other and far busier end of Chickamauga Lake.

148 DAYMARK 514.2

Here, corn and pasture fields edge the water and farm buildings can be seen in the distance.

After another mile, you will be greeted with a sweeping view of the Cumberland Plateau.

DAYMARK 518.0

This is the new Tennessee 30 bridge which replaced the Washington Ferry. Called the William Jennings Bryan Memorial Highway, this highway links Dayton with Athens and Decatur.

For the next few miles, the river narrows even more and you are likely to feel an intimacy with the bordering landscape that you haven't experienced for quite some time.

MILE 523.2

From here, you can see the cooling towers at TVA's Watts Bar nuclear power plant. After another three miles, the plant will be in full view.

MILE 529.9

This is Watts Bar Dam. This complex is unique because it's the only TVA site shared by a hydroelectric dam, a coal-fired power plant which is now inactive, and a nuclear power plant of which only one unit is operating.

Watts Bar Dam is 112 feet high and with a length of only 2,960 feet, is the shortest of all the mainstream dams on the Tennessee. Construction began in 1939 and was completed in 1942.

The lock, on the east end of the dam, is one of the smallest on the river. Also, you will notice on the official charts that it has only three floating mooring posts at port and one at starboard.

The highway on top of the dam is Tennessee 68 which links Spring City to the west with Tennessee 58 and I-75 to the east.

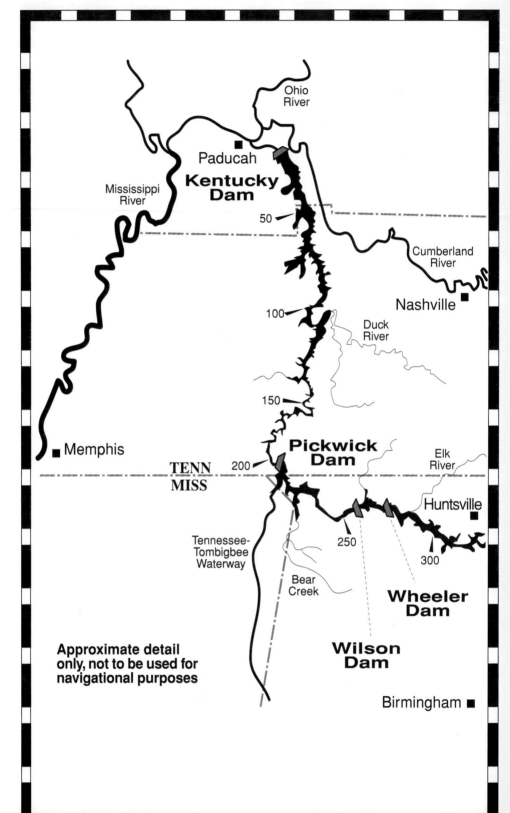

The
Tennessee River

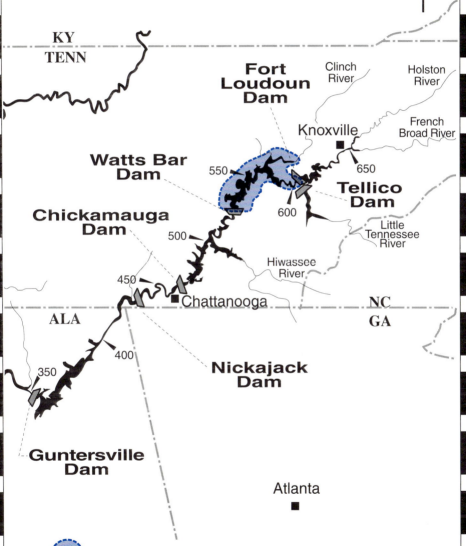

N

KY
TENN

Fort
Loudoun
Dam

Clinch
River

Holston
River

Knoxville

French
Broad River

Watts Bar
Dam

550

650

Tellico
Dam

600

Chickamauga
Dam

500

Little
Tennessee
River

450

Hiwassee
River

Chattanooga

NC
GA

ALA

400

Nickajack
Dam

350

Guntersville
Dam

Atlanta

Watts Bar Lake

As you clear the lock, you will quickly understand why Watts Bar is considered by many to be the most beautiful lake on the Tennessee. Beyond the large expanses of water are islands then low hills covered with farms and forest. And always in the distance are the Cumberland Mountains.

Watts Bar also is the least used lake. Chattanooga boaters are drawn to Chickamauga Lake because of its closeness. Knoxville boaters have the same advantage in their use of Fort Loudoun Lake and Tellico Lake. In between is Watts Bar, unspoiled, uncrowded, and far from industry and large population centers.

Increasingly, however, Watts Bar is being discovered and each year more land is developed and more homes built.

MILE 530.4
FUEL
RESTAURANT
LODGING
ANCHORAGE

If after locking through you wish to rest awhile, have a good meal, or stay overnight, turn to port about a half mile upstream from the lock and enter the embayment with the aerial power crossing.

To the left after the embayment splits you will see the dock belonging to Watts Bar Resort. The 200-acre resort has a range of facilities and services including cabins, a swimming pool, tennis courts, hiking trails, and nearby golf courses.

Because the dock's primary purpose is to serve the resort's guests, it's quite busy between June and Labor Day. The resort does its best, however, to accommodate transient boaters who wish to stay overnight but sometimes space isn't available. So call first. There is gas and 30 amp electrical service.

A courtesy car will take you to the restaurant which offers a variety of dishes from a general menu for both lunch and dinner. Or if you prefer to walk in pleasant surroundings, the distance is only a bit more than a mile. For more information, call 423-365-9595.

Anchorage: As you leave the small embayment on which the Watts Bar Resort dock is located, turn sharply to port into a larger embayment that splits into two coves. Water depth will be about 18 feet at normal pool at the entrance and until you reach the split but will decrease rather quickly after you enter each cove. The moderately steep banks are wooded, and there are no structures, and you will be protected from all but northeast winds. The cove to port offers the best wind protection. West winds may affect you in the cove to starboard unless you anchor in its upper reaches.

MILE 531.0
ANCHORAGE

This anchorage is off the large Lowe Branch embayment. To avoid shallow water on your port side, favor the center as you enter Lowe Branch. Turn into the first cove at port. You can easily identify it because there's a power line on the hill at the far end. Water depth will be about 25 feet at normal pool until you are about three-fourths into the embayment then gradually becomes less. The completely wooded banks are nearly level to moderately steep, there are no structures, there's plenty of space on which to swing on one anchor, and you will be well protected from all but north winds. By anchoring just inside the entrance in deeper water you will have a fine view of the lake.

MILE 532.3
MARINA
LODGING
ANCHORAGE

Not until you enter Piney River will you discover that it's one of the Tennessee's hidden delights. Turn to port just below Daymark 532.8 and follow the marked channel. Within a mile, the channel gradually turns to starboard, passes between two peninsulas and under an aerial power crossing, then turns sharply to port. There, you will be greeted by a mile wide expanse of exceptionally clear and tranquil water dotted with islands and surrounded with the beautiful foothills of the Cumberland Mountains.

Continue straight ahead for about two miles. There, the channel splits. Turn to starboard here, go past the first red buoy, then steer toward the second one. If you have trouble spotting it, head for the distant water tank on land, a compass heading of about 305 degrees, which is almost in line with the second buoy. After you pass a small island at port, turn sharply to port past two sets of buoys. Rhea Harbor Resort & Marina will be directly in front of you.

Rhea Harbor Resort & Marina
385 Lakeshire Drive
Spring City, Tennessee 37381
1-800-382-6851

Open all year, 8AM until 7PM from March 1 to November 1, and 8AM until 5PM and closed on Sunday for the remainder of the year. Can accommodate boats up to 55 feet. Has several transient slips and 20 amp electrical service. Has gas. Has launch ramp and facilities for repairing gas engines. A diesel mechanic is on call. Has ice and a limited selection of boating supplies. Can arrange transportation to nearby Spring City if you wish to buy groceries. Monitors channel 16.

Accepts MasterCard, Visa, Discover, and American Express credit cards.

Lodging: The marina has 12 cabins on the premises with 1-3 bedrooms. The rates are "very low for anyone wishing to overwinter."

A convenient anchorage is just beyond Piney River Daymark 3.4, the only Daymark on the river. It's on the point of land at port you pass enroute to Rhea Harbor Resort & Marina. A short distance beyond the Daymark is a green buoy. Go past it and turn to port toward the embayment ahead of you. Water depth will be at least 25 feet at normal pool until you reach the narrow part of the embayment where it begins to gradually decrease to about 18 feet. The banks here are fairly steep and wooded and there are no structures. Wind protection is good from all directions except north. If you stay overnight here, the morning view across the river's wide expanse to the north is particularly appealing.

MILE 536.0

At this point upstream from Daymark 534.3, the navigation channel swings sharply to starboard. A marked secondary channel indicated on the navigation charts is straight ahead. Although it will cut three miles from your trip, the channel is very narrow and is only about seven feet deep at normal pool. So if your boat is longer than about 40 feet, you will probably feel more comfortable following the main navigation channel around Gillespie Bend.

MILE 538.0

The small island at port after you pass Daymark 537.5 is a rarity along the Tennessee River because it has a sandy beach. Appropriately called Sand Island, it's a favorite place for boaters to congregate on summer weekends. If you want to get close to the island, turn toward it just as soon as you pass the first green buoy. Use caution if you approach the other three sides of the island where the water is much shallower.

DAYMARK 541.6
ANCHORAGES

Turn immediately to starboard past this Daymark and you will be entering Pearl Harbor. It consists of four coves all of which are exceedingly fine anchorages.

Everything here is visually soft. The banks rise gradually from the water and the forest is a mixture of pines and hardwoods. Even in the upper reaches of each cove, you can expect a water depth of at least 10 feet and protection from wind from any direction. There are a few houses on the southern most cove, but they tend to blend into the landscape rather than intrude. Pearl Harbor's reputation has spread, however, and on summer weekends it can be crowded.

MILE 542.3
MARINA
LODGING

If you favor a quiet environment, you might want to consider Eden Resort Marina. The entrance is just past Daymark 541.6 but on the opposite bank and is marked with a small sign. You can see part of the facility from the main river. As you approach, you will see a second dock. The fuel pumps are on the left and nearer the bank. You won't be able to see them until you clear the end of the dock.

Eden Resort Marina
653 Scenic Lakeview Drive
Spring city, Tennessee 37381
423-365-6929

Open all year, 8AM until 6PM. Owner is always on site. Can accommodate boats to 50 feet. Has no transient slips but arrangements can be made. Reservations are necessary.

Has 30 amp electrical service. Water depth at the fuel dock is 12 feet at normal pool. Has gas. Has launch ramp. Has mechanic on call. Has showers, ice, snacks, and some boating supplies. Grocery store is 3 miles away. Monitors channel 16. Accepts MasterCard and Visa credit cards.

Lodging: The resort marina has trailers and efficiency apartments. Reservations are necessary to rent these units.

MILE 543.5

The silo at starboard is a reminder that at one time, much of the land now under water was farmland. As each dam on the Tennessee was built, hundreds of farm families faced the grim reality that homes and land that had been in the family for generations would soon be lost forever. For those here, that was in 1942 when Watts Bar Dam was completed.

Most families realized the benefits that developing the Tennessee River would bring and resigned themselves to relocating. But others didn't.

Twentieth Century Fox used the dilemma as the basis for producing *Wild River,* a highly acclaimed movie made in 1960 starring Lee Remick and Montgomery Clift. It's a fictional account of a TVA land buyer's efforts to persuade an elderly matriarch to leave her home and property which was soon to be inundated. The movie was made on the Hiawassee River near Charleston, Tennessee.

DAYMARK 543.9

This is Half-Moon Cutoff. It will reduce your route by almost two miles. But if you're not in a hurry, you may want to follow the original river channel and perhaps explore White Creek, the large embayment at port just before the turn and Phillips Branch which is straight ahead as you make the turn.

MILE 546.7
ANCHORAGE

This embayment is on the far bank directly in front of you as you leave the cutoff and the first one downstream from the First Class harbor shown on the official charts. Soon after entering, turn into the cove at starboard. Water depth will be about 10 feet at normal pool when you come to within about 50 feet of the wooded and nearly level bank. There are two houses at the far end of the embayment. You will have plenty of space here for swinging on one anchor and be well protected from all winds, particulary from the south.

MILE 547.6
ANCHORAGE

To reach this anchorage, round the point, pass Daymark 547.5, and enter the embayment. Steer slightly to starboard to enter the much larger cove. As you proceed to a point even with a small cove to starboard, water depth will be about 18 feet at normal pool. There's plenty of space to swing on one anchor. Almost all of the nearly level to moderately steep bank is wooded. One house is at the end of the enbayment. You will, however, be well protected from all winds and have a nice view of the main lake.

MILE 547.7
MARINA
RESTAURANT
LODGING

Directly across the lake and marked by a sign is the entrance to Blue Springs Resort and Marina. You must be well inside this embayment before you can see the marina at port. To reach the fuel dock, pass the marina then come in on the back side near the store and office building.

Blue Springs Resort & Marina
Route 2, Box 324
Ten Mile, Tennessee 37880
423-376-7298

Open all year, 7AM until 9PM April 1 to Labor Day, then 8AM until 6PM for the remainder of the year. Can accommodate boats to 70 feet. Has 8 transient slips. Has double 30 amp and 50 amp electrical service. Water depth at the fuel dock is 19 feet at normal pool. Has gas and diesel fuel. Has showers, laundromat, pump out, ice, snacks, some groceries, and some boating supplies. Has facilities for repairing both gas and diesel engines. Has launch ramp and 18-ton lift for boats up to 48 feet. Courtesy car is available for driving to nearby grocery. Monitors channel 16. Accepts MasterCard, Visa, and Discover credit cards.

Restaurant: The Blue Springs Restaurant which overlooks the marina is open from March to November and serves breakfast, lunch and dinner.

Lodging: The marina has 7 housekeeping cabins on the premises with amenities including cable TV.

Some boaters become a bit confused as they leave this marina and mistakenly turn too soon to starboard on their way back to the main lake. If you go to the side of the embayment opposite the marina before turning, you will be able to easily retrace your route.

DAYMARK 548.2
MARINA
RESTAURANT
LODGING

A mile upstream from Blue Springs Resort & Marina is the entrance to Gordon Branch and a sign indicating Bayside Marina & Resort. Soon after you enter the embayment, you will see the marina in the distance at port. As you move toward it, slow down to no-wake speed.

Bayside Marina & Resort
134 Bayside Drive
Ten Mile, Tennessee 37880
423-376-7031

Open 7AM until 9PM March 15 to November 15. Can accommodate boats up to 60 feet.

Has 4 transient slips and 20 amp electrical service. Water depth at the fuel dock is 15 feet at normal pool. Has gas and the largest fuel dock on Watts Bar Lake. Has launch ramp, ice, and showers. Has light groceries including milk and bread. Also, a convenience store is a mile away. "We can usually get people what they need." Has some boating supplies. Monitors channel 16. Accepts MasterCard, Visa, and Discover credit cards.

Restaurant: The Ship and Shore Restaurant on the hill behind the marina is popular among many area boaters. It's open 7AM until 9PM every day from March 15 to November 15, and serves from a general menu.

Lodging: The marina has lakefront cabins and motel rooms that can be rented by the day or week.

DAYMARK 550.4

This is the entrance to Thief Neck Cutoff. If you use it, be sure to carefully follow the channel markers. The very shallow water outside them is particularly unforgiving.

**MILE 551.0
MARINA**

Using the cutoff will save you about five miles but in doing so you'll miss some nice scenery and a marina. Also, you may wish to hike a 6.4 mile trail that loops Thief Neck Island. The trail begins just inside the first large cove soon after you pass the cutoff channel and begin to circle the island. Look for the trail sign at starboard about a third of the way into the embayment. As you come abreast of the sign, water depth will be about 20 feet at normal pool. Space is a bit tight here so a second anchor may be needed for larger boats. Also, you will be exposed to southwest winds.

On the other side of the lake is Ferguson Branch, location of Harbour Point Marina.

The marina is clearly visible from a considerable distance and offers overnight boaters an exceptionally fine view of Watts Bar Lake. You will see the fuel dock just after you pass the end of the first dock.

Harbour Point Marina
184 Marina Bay Road
Rockwood, Tennessee 37854
423-354-2974

Open all year, 8AM until 4:30PM. Can accommodate boats up to 120 feet. Has 500 feet of docking space available to transients. Has 30 amp and 50 amp electrical power. Water depth at the fuel dock is 17 feet at normal pool. Has gas and diesel fuel. Has 35-ton lift. A mechanic on duty can handle most repairs. Has showers and some boating supplies. Has ice and snacks. Arrangements for a rental car can be made for travel to Rockwood six miles away. Monitors channel 16. Accepts MasterCard and Visa credit cards.

DAYMARK 558.2
ANCHORAGE

If you're looking for a more open anchorage offering a fine view of islands and the lake, this is worth a look. Go upstream from this Daymark about 150 feet to avoid a narrow shoal then turn sharply to port until you're even with the midpoint between the first two islands at starboard. The water is at least 10 feet deep at normal pool. There are no structures, the wooded banks are nearly level to moderately steep, and there's plenty of space for swinging on one anchor. For greater wind protection, you can move deeper into the embayment past the islands. Swinging space, however, is limited and you may feel more comfortable using a stern anchor if the weather gets nasty.

MILE 561.3
ANCHORAGE

This embayment is identified on the official charts as a First Class harbor. When you enter, avoid shallow water by favoring the downstream side. There are two coves. Turn slightly to port to enter the wider and more spacious cove. A short distance beyond the split, water depth will be about 22 feet at normal pool. There are houses ahead and at starboard. The mostly wooded banks range from gently sloping to fairly steep. You should have enough space for swinging on one anchor and there's good wind protection from every direction except west. The cove at port is slightly shallower but more sheltered and secluded.

DAYMARK 564.6

At this point, you can see the stacks of TVA's Kingston power plant rising above the hills.

DAYMARK 567.6

Here, the Tennessee is joined by another of its major tributaries, the Clinch River. It's navigable for 61 miles to Clinton, Tennessee.

The Clinch begins in southwest Virginia then flows southward into Tennessee where it forms Norris Lake behind TVA's Norris Dam. This lake, largest of the 24 tributary lakes in the Tennessee River system, is 129 miles long.

Past Clinton, the Clinch flows east of Oak Ridge where it's stopped by TVA's Melton Hill Dam. Just above Kingston, it's joined by the Emory River which is navigable for 12 miles.

Kingston traces its history to the increasing number of early pioneers who wished to live close to Fort Southwest Point. The fort, an army garrison from 1792 to 1807, was on top of the hill ahead and at port where the Tennessee is joined by the Clinch River. Since 1974, many archaeological investigations have been conducted at and near the site of the fort. A partial reconstruction has recently been built on the original foundation.

Downtown Kingston is easy to access. Enter the Clinch River just above Daymark 567.6 and go upstream about a mile. At starboard and at the far end of a two story apartment building is a dock. Near the dock and on the river bank is a sign reading "Downtown Dock."

Water depth at the dock is about 10 feet at normal pool. Because of the dock's short length and limited support, use special care in docking if your boat is longer than about 30 feet. A better choice might be to anchor away from the dock and use a dinghy.

The reward for such effort, however, is convenience. Within three blocks of the dock are a grocery, hardware store, bank, and several other businesses. Also, several historic structures are in or near the downtown area including the Roane County Courthouse at the corner of Kentucky and Cumberland streets. It's one of only seven remaining antebellum courthouses in Tennessee.

MILE 568.0

After you return to the junction of the Tennessee and the Clinch, you'll see the Kingston-Decatur bridge, Tennessee 58. Upstream from the bridge are many nice homes, mostly because Kingston is only 35 miles from downtown Knoxville via I-40.

MILE 569.5

Here, the river splits to flow around both sides of Long Island, a wildlife area and the largest of several that dot the landscape for nearly six more miles. The navigation channel veers to port.

From here to Fort Loudoun Dam, the navigation channel continues to be quite narrow. So be particularly careful to follow the channel markers.

Most homes and other signs of civilization fade away in favor of bluffs, densely wooded hills, and rolling pasture land.

MILE 575.8 ANCHORAGE

This embayment is Little Paint Rock Creek. Stay to center upon entering where water will be about 12 feet at normal pool. About a half mile up the embayment where there's a small cove at port, water depth will be about 12 feet. The few houses along the wooded banks are mostly hidden. This long embayment is oriented northwest and southwest. So winds from those directions may bother you. But there is plenty of space to swing on one anchor.

DAYMARK 583.1

Ahead is the I-75 bridge. This highway begins at the Canadian border at Sault Ste. Marie, Michigan, and links Detroit, Cincinnati, and Lexington, with Knoxville, Chattanooga, Atlanta, Tampa, and Miami.

DAYMARK 589.1

Here, the topography changes again as the bluffs give way to low and flat banks. Fields extend almost to the water's edge.

MILE 591.3

This is the Southern Railway Bridge and ahead of you is the Loudon County Memorial Highway Bridge, U.S. 11, that leads into downtown Loudon.

Settlers, many of whom were English soldiers, founded the town in 1790. Originally known as Blairsville, Loudon later became important as a transportation and commercial center. Today, the city has a population of about 4,000. A walking tour of Loudon includes more than a dozen historic buildings.

There's considerable industry along most of the river bank at port for the next two miles. So stay alert for possible commercial tow traffic.

MILE 601.0

The wide water at starboard is the former mouth of the Little Tennessee River. Look closely through the trees and you may get a glimpse of Tellico Dam. Most of the dam's 3,200-foot length consists of an earthen embankment.

The dam became the center of a bitter controversy soon after TVA announced plans to build it. Sportsmen protested because the dam would destroy a clear and free flowing river long favored for its fishing. The Cherokee Indians objected because it would destroy their ancestral burying grounds and cover sites of their former villages. Environmentalists took the position that the dam not only wasn't needed but also that it would destroy the habitat of the Snail Darter, a dwarf freshwater fish.

TVA insisted that building the dam and creating Tellico Lake would further enhance economic development and prevent millions of dollars in flood damage downstream.

Despite the objections, TVA began construction in 1967 but was legally forced to stop when the dam was nearly finished. Eventually, an Act of Congress signed by President Carter allowed TVA to complete the project in 1979 and create Tellico Lake.

MILE 602.3

This is Fort Loudoun Dam, the last of the nine dams on the Tennessee River. It's 122 feet high and 4,190 feet long. Construction began in 1940 and was completed in 1943. The lock, second highest on the river, is on the south end of the dam, your starboard side.

As with the Watts Bar lock, this lock has only three floating mooring posts at port and one at starboard. So be prepared to lock through on your port side if the lockmaster requests it.

The highways crossing the dam are U.S. 321 and Tennessee 95 which link I-75, I-40, and Lenoir City to the west with Maryville and Alcoa to the east.

This lake is a water playground for both local boaters and those from towns and cities as far away as Atlanta. As a result, the lower end of the lake can be extremely busy on summer weekends.

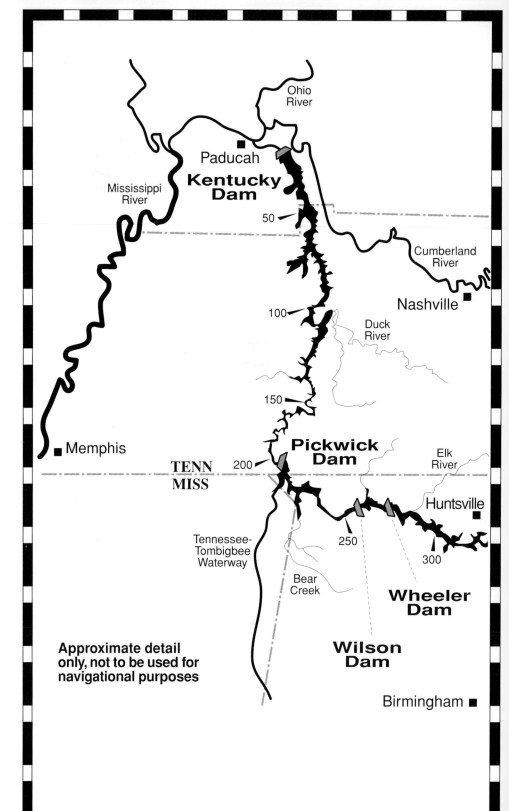

Ohio River

Paducah

Kentucky Dam

Mississippi River

50

Cumberland River

Nashville

100

Duck River

150

Pickwick Dam

Elk River

TENN
MISS

200

Huntsville

250

Tennessee-Tombigbee Waterway

300

Wheeler Dam

Memphis

Bear Creek

Wilson Dam

Approximate detail only, not to be used for navigational purposes

Birmingham

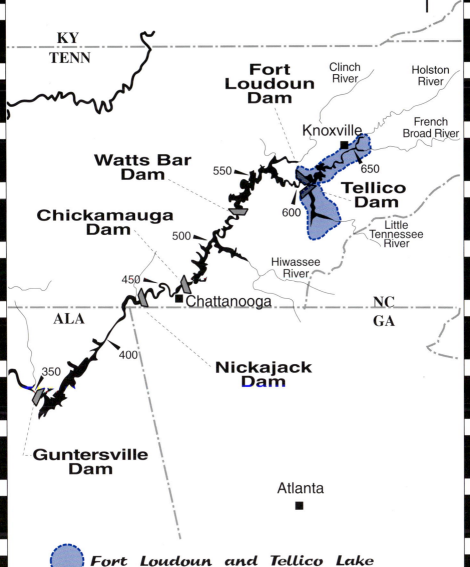

The
Tennessee
River

N

KY
TENN

Clinch
River

Holston
River

**Fort
Loudoun
Dam**

Knoxville

French
Broad River

**Watts Bar
Dam**

550

650

**Tellico
Dam**

600

**Chickamauga
Dam**

500

Little
Tennessee
River

450

Hiwassee
River

Chattanooga

NC

ALA

GA

400

**Nickajack
Dam**

350

**Guntersville
Dam**

Atlanta

Fort Loudoun and Tellico Lake

Fort Loudoun is the last lake on the Tennessee River. Although you won't see a wide expanse of water when you leave the lock, there's much more upstream than what first appears. If it's a clear day, you will be able to see the dim outline of the Smoky Mountains.

At starboard is the entrance to a short canal leading to Tellico Lake.

Compared to the main Tennessee River, the water in Tellico Lake is clearer and colder. That's because the Little Tennessee River begins in the Great Smoky Mountains. There are no large towns and almost no industry or intensive agriculture in its watershed. Also, much of the water tends to be deep, even well into most embayments.

The scenery becomes increasingly interesting as you cruise farther up the lake and get much closer to the mountains. Also, a trip up the Tellico will provide you with a fine opportunity to gain a much better understanding of the role of the Cherokee Indians in our Nation's history.

The following entries relate to the Little Tennessee River or LTR from which Tellico Lake was formed.

Caution! If you require a vertical clearance of more than 42 feet at normal pool, you won't be able to pass under the highway bridge that spans the canal between Fort Loudoun Lake and Tellico Lake. If you require more than 35 feet, you won't be able to go any farther than the fixed span CSX Railroad bridge at LTR Mile 18.6.

LTR MILE 3.4

The three silos at starboard are another reminder that much of what is under you was farmland that was flooded when Tellico Dam was built. You will see more silos as you cruise up the river. Behind the silos is one of several saddle dams. These were built where the landscape was lower than the lake level was to be after Tellico Dam was completed.

**LTR MILE 5.5
ANCHORAGE**

To port across from three silos is a long embayment locally known as Power Line Cove because of the aerial power crossings at its upper end. If you are in a sailboat, take note that these crossings provide only 38 feet of vertical clearance. You can expect a water depth of about 15 feet at normal pool two-thirds of the distance between the crossings and the end of the embayment. The nearly flat to moderately steep banks are wooded and there are no structures. There is, however, a narrow road at the end of the embayment used by fishermen. You will have plenty of space to swing on one anchor and be protected from all but northwest winds. One reason this is a popular anchorage is because the embayment is curved which keeps the often busy main lake out of sight for anyone anchored at the far end.

LTR MILE 7.0

Beginning here at starboard, the bank is covered with fine homes. Many feature interesting architecture and landscaping. The Tellico Lake area is becoming increasingly popular with people from northern states who choose to retire here because of the water, mountains, moderate climate, and nearby Knoxville.

**LTR MILE 8.3
ANCHORAGE**

At port is Sinking Creek, an attractive anchorage that allows you a fine opportunity to anchor about a half mile away from the main lake. Follow the embayment around the turn to where it widens. Anchor in the area opposite a farm road which skirts the southern side. Water depth here will be about 12 feet at normal pool. The wooded banks give way in the distance to a farm. There's plenty of space on which to swing on one anchor and you will be well protected from all wind except possibly from the east.

LTR MILE 10.2

You can save about two miles if you take the secondary channel leading off to port but be sure you stay between the channel markers.

LTR MILE 16.1

At starboard is an industrial area. As you enter this wide area of the lake and look ahead, you will get your first good look at the distant and majestic Smoky Mountains.

**LTR MILE 18.1
ANCHORAGE**

Just beyond this Daymark at port is a convenient anchorage, especially for sailboats that can't pass under the bridges ahead. After entering the embayment, proceed to where it widens. Water depth there and in the center is about 25 feet at normal pool then becomes a more ideal anchoring depth of about 10 feet just a short distance to port. The nearly level to moderately steep banks are wooded except for an open field. There's plenty of space on which to swing on one anchor. You will be protected from all but southwest winds and have a good view of the lake.

The first bridge is the CSX railroad bridge. The second is the U.S. 411 bridge. This highway links many towns on the east side of the Tennessee River with Chattanooga to the south and Knoxville to the north.

LTR 19.2

Immediately after passing under the bridges, you will be entering one of the Tennessee Valley's most historic areas.

For an interesting side trip, turn to starboard here on the Tellico River. After cruising up the Tellico for a bit more than a mile you will pass under the Vonore-Toqua highway bridge. Beyond it and past three green buoys, you will be curving to port and passing behind a small island. After clearing the island, you will see the impressive Sequoyah Birthplace Memorial and Museum at the top of a grassy hill. At the bottom of the hill is a "T" dock that provides about 20 feet of docking space. The dock has limited support so approach it slowly and carefully. Water depth at the dock is about 15 feet at normal pool.

The museum opened in 1986 as a tribute to Sequoyah and the Indians who lived in the Little Tennessee River Valley. Owned by the Eastern Band of Cherokee Indians, it's Tennessee's only tribally owned enterprise.

Inside are exhibits that retrace 8,000 years of continuous habitation in the valley. During the 18th century, the valley was the center of Cherokee political and cultural activity. It was in this environment that Sequoyah was born and later dedicated himself to the tedious task of creating a written language for the Cherokees. He was so successful that the entire Cherokee Nation became literate. Even today, the syllabary is used by the more than 10,000 people who speak the Cherokee Language. Sequoyah's accomplishments became so widely known that many places and things have been named after him including the Sequoyah trees in California.

Near the museum is the Cherokee Memorial where the remains of 18th century Cherokees were placed after being excavated during archaeological studies conducted before Tellico Lake was created.

Along with the museum is a large gift shop with a wide selection of contemporary Cherokee arts and crafts and books on Cherokee culture and history. For more information, call 423-884-6246.

Before leaving the museum, you may want to consider walking the 1.6 miles to Fort Loudoun described below. That's particularly true if your boat is too large to tie up to the small dock at the fort.

LTR MILE 19.2

Before you do, however, you might consider continuing up the Tellico River and enjoying the scenery. Although much of the area is still a mixture of forest and farmland, residential development is increasing. As the official charts indicate, the channel is marked up to where Ballplay Creek joins the river, a distance of about five miles upriver from the Sequoyah Museum. The Tellico continues in a southerly direction beyond that point. But if it's too narrow for you, turn up the relatively wide water of Ballplay Creek at port. After about a mile, shallower water and a low highway bridge prevent larger boats from going farther.

LTR MILE 19.5

Ahead is the site of Fort Loudoun. This fort helped Great Britain prevent the French from penetrating the Appalachian region during the French and Indian War.

It was built during the winter of 1756, and named after John Campbell, the fourth Earl of Loudoun, who was the British Commander-in-Chief in North America from 1756 to 1758.

But tragedy struck in less than two years. A breakdown in relations between the British and the Cherokee Nation resulted in 23

Indians being executed in South Carolina in late 1759.

The Cherokees, who had become anti-British, cut the fort's supply line in March, 1760. Diplomatic efforts to free the fort failed. With food rations nearly gone, the commander asked the Cherokees for terms of surrender. Then on the morning of August 9, the garrison of 180 men and 60 women and children left the fort and traveled some distance before making camp at nightfall.

At sunrise the next morning, the Cherokees attacked the camp and killed almost every officer plus 20 to 30 others. The survivors were taken as slaves and eventually ransomed.

Across from the reconstructed fort on your port side is the site of the Tellico Blockhouse. Although built in 1794 for military reasons, its primary purpose was to protect the Cherokees from continued advances of white settlers into the valley.

Two years later, the U.S. Government built a trading post there to dispense supplies to the Cherokees. Also, the War Department's Indian agent was stationed there until 1801. Four years later, the treaty allowing the United States to gain title to all of what is now Middle Tennessee also called for the blockhouse to be removed. Today, all that remains is an archaeological ruin.

There are docks at the fort and the blockhouse. Although at normal pool the water is deep enough at both of them for large boats, the docks aren't large enough for docking boats more than about 20 feet in length. Longer docks are planned but until they are built, the only alternative is to anchor nearby and use a dinghy.

LTR MILE 20.1
MARINA
RESTAURANT

As you pass the blockhouse site you will see the marked entrance to Nine Mile Creek. A short distance up the marked channel and around the turn is Tellico Harbor Marina.

Tellico Harbor Marina
1000 Marina Harbor Drive
Maryville, Tennessee 37801
423-856-6806

Open all year, 9AM until 7PM every day. Can accommodate boats to 80 feet. Has 10 transient slips. Has 30 amp and 50 amp electrical power. Water depth at the fuel dock is 18 feet at normal pool. Has gas. Has ice and pump out and offers a full range of boat repairs. "We can do anything to any boat except interiors." Has 25-ton lift. Is 22 miles from Knoxville Airport and 42 miles from Gatlinburg. Transportation from the marina can be arranged. Monitors channel 16. Accepts MasterCard and Visa credit cards.

Restaurant: The restaurant on the premises is seasonal and is open from Memorial Day to Labor Day.

LTR MILE 20.2
ANCHORAGE

As you pass the fort, the water quickly widens and you will be presented with the most magnificent view yet of the Smoky Mountains. If no heavy weather is expected and you wish to anchor out, turn to starboard just past the fort to a point about 300 feet from the bank. Water depth there will be about 20 feet at normal pool.

LTR MILE 20.5

To help keep you on course as you leave the fort and start across the wide water, steer toward the diamond shaped marker on the bank about three miles ahead.

For the next nine miles you will feel as close to nature as anywhere else on the entire

Tennessee. All of the land on both sides and extending upward into the mountains is part of the Cherokee National Forest.

You will, however, need to pay special attention to the channel markers. They are harder to see because they are much smaller than those on the main navigation channel. Also, they tend to be farther apart. For that reason, the official charts will be particularly helpful along this last stretch of the river.

LTR MILE 24.5

Soon after you pass the diamond shaped marker, the river begins a horseshoe bend. About two-thirds of the way through the bend and at starboard is a group of round upright stone markers at the end of a narrow peninsula. This is the site of the Cherokee town of Chota. Each of the stones represents a Cherokee clan, those of Deer, Wild Potato, Wolf, Paint, Bird, Long Hair, and Blue.

Farther away and to the right of the Chota marker and best seen with binoculars is the marker indicating the site of the Cherokee town of Tanasi. The town gained prominence in 1721 when its civil chief was elected the first "emperor of the Cherokee Nation." From then until 1730, Tanasi was capital of the Cherokee Nation.

About the same time, the name Tanasi was applied to the river. The first recorded spelling of the word "Tennessee," a variation of Tanasi, was on a map prepared in 1762 by Lt. Henry Timberlake. In 1796, the name Tennessee was selected from among several possibilities as the most appropriate for the Nation's 16th state.

LTR MILE 28.6

Just downstream of where Four Mile Creek enters the river is a high cliff. The clearly vis-**177**

ible rock folds are evidence of the powerful geological forces that shaped and formed this land millions of years ago.

LTR MILE 29.6

The official navigation channel ends just before you reach this aerial power crossing at the top of the picturesque bluff of brown and red rock. When the water level is at or near normal pool, travel is possible for about two more miles upstream. Follow the natural curve of the river as it curves to port.

You would be wise, however, to stop at the piers of the abandoned trestle at Mile 31.1. Beyond it, water depth is more unpredictable because of varying amounts of water released from Chilhowee Dam at Mile 33.4.

If you do go as far as the piers, proceed about midway between the bank at port and the islands and dead trees at starboard which mark the other side of the original river channel.

Whether you stop at Mile 29.6 or at the piers, the southern end of Chilhowee Mountain rising more than 1,400 feet above you serves as an appropriate exclamation point to some of the finest scenery on the Tennessee.

MILE 602.6
MARINA
RESTAURANTS

As you leave Fort Loudoun lock, look ahead and slightly to port. You will see Ft. Loudoun Marina. The fuel dock will be visible as soon as you clear the right end of the large dock with covered slips.

Ft. Loudoun Marina
5200 City Park Drive, Unit 101
Lenoir City, Tennessee 37772
423-986-5536 or 423-523-6358
423-986-1239 (Fax)

Open all year, 9AM until 8PM, April 1 to October 1, 9AM until 5PM for the remainder of the year. Can accommodate boats up to 70 feet. Has eight transient slips and 30 amp and 50 amp electrical service. Water depth at the fuel dock is 20 feet at normal pool. Has gas and diesel fuel. Has launch ramp, ice, showers, and laundromat. The "Captain's Locker" serves breakfast, a wide range of sandwiches, and a dinner buffet on summer weekends. Snacks and a few boating supplies also are available. Complete grocery service in nearby Lenoir City is accessible by taxi or by transportation that can be arranged with the marina. Rental cars are available at the Knoxville airport 18 miles away and in Lenoir City. Monitors channel 16. Accepts MasterCard, Visa, and Discover credit cards.

Adjoining the marina is Reed Marine Service with service facilities for engine overhauling and mechanical, electrical, and plumbing repairs. For more information call 423-986-4433.

Restaurant: The third part of the marina complex is the popular Calhoun's Restaurant, one of five in the Knoxville area. Built partly on pilings and providing a commanding view of the marina, it serves from a general menu but is famous for its barbequed ribs. It also offers both indoor and outdoor dining. For more information, call 423-673-3366.

MILE 603.0

For the next few miles, you'll see many fine homes, perhaps more than anywhere else on the entire river.

MILE 608.0

Here, the river presents an illusion by appearing to end about two miles ahead. Not until you get much closer do you discover that it turns sharply to starboard and flows past Saltpeter Bluff.

DAYMARK 616.1
MARINAS
ANCHORAGE

Here, the water quickly widens. Ahead are two low highway bridges. Beyond the second one which leads to the Sinking Creek embayment are two marinas, Concord Marina and Fox Road Marina. As you get closer, you'll see their names painted on the bridge.

Caution! Vertical clearance of this bridge is 17.0 feet at normal pool. Also, both marinas are affected by wakes from passing boats. So make sure you watch yours.

Concord Marina is at starboard soon after you pass under the bridge.

Concord Marina
1100 Fox Road
Knoxville, Tennessee 37922
423-966-5831

Open all year, 9AM until 8PM, April 1 to Memorial Day; 9AM until 9PM Memorial Day through Labor Day; 9AM until 6PM on Friday, Saturday, and Sunday from Labor Day to November 30; 9AM until 5:30PM Monday through Friday for remainder of the year. Can accommodate boats up to 55 feet. Has three transient slips and twin 30 amp electrical service. Water depth at the fuel dock is 20 feet at normal pool. Has gas. Has public launch ramp. Can perform repairs on gas engines. Has facilities for hauling out houseboats up to 50 feet and cruisers up to 38 feet. Has ice and expanded snack service including salads, sandwiches, and breakfast on weekends. Has some boat supplies. Accepts MasterCard and Visa credit cards.

Fox Road Marina is about a mile beyond Concord Marina and on the opposite side.

Fox Road Marina
1100 Fox Road
Knoxville, Tennessee 37922
423-966-9422

Open all year, 9AM until 8PM Memorial Day through Labor Day; 9AM until 5PM, Labor day to November 30; 9AM until 5:30PM Monday through Friday for remainder of the year. Can accommodate boats up to 60 feet. Has three transient slips and twin 30 amp electrical service. Water depth at the fuel dock is 15 feet at normal pool. Has gas. Has launch ramp. Can perform engine repairs including generators and outdrives. Has ice, snacks, sandwiches, and some boating supplies. Marina manager will try to accommodate you if you need complete grocery service in nearby Concord or wish to visit local restaurants. Arrangements for car rental can be made. Accepts MasterCard and Visa credit cards.

Anchorage: Beyond Fox Road Marina, Sinking Creek becomes somewhat narrower and is eventually crossed by the Pellissippi Parkway. This entire area is suitable for anchoring. Water depth will range from 10 to 18 feet. Wind protection is minimal but is best from north and south. There's plenty of space for swinging on one anchor. There are houses and docks at port but none at starboard.

DAYMARK 618.5 ANCHORAGE

The small embayment just before you reach this Daymark offers you a chance to get off the main river either for a short time or possibly overnight. Water depth in the center is about 20 feet at normal pool. There are no houses on the open banks devoted mostly to pasture but you will be exposed to west and northwest winds. There's enough space for swinging on one anchor.

MILE 620.2
ANCHORAGE

Just past Daymark 619.6 at starboard is the entrance to Poland Creek which is further identified by a sign advertising the Poland Creek Nursery. Water depth as you enter the creek at center will be about 20 feet at normal pool. After a half mile, the creek widens considerably and you will be able to see a TVA recreation area. Because of the boat ramp ahead, the best place to anchor is at starboard in front of the campground. Water depth will be about 10 feet as you come abreast of the campground then becomes more shallow as you move farther into the embayment. The general environment can be busy, especially on weekends. Also, the west side is being developed for residential housing. Yet, farmland on the east side of Poland Creek is easy on the eyes, there's plenty of room for swinging on one anchor, and you will have fairly good wind protection particularly from the south.

DAYMARK 624.5
ANCHORAGE

At the end of Sheep Pen bluff and just beyond this Daymark is Caney Branch. Because of several nearby houses, you might not want to stay here overnight. But this embayment does give you a chance to get off the main river and there's enough space for you to swing on one anchor. Water depth will be about 15 feet at normal pool up to almost where the embayment splits. Wind protection is good from every direction except north.

DAYMARK 625.6
MARINA

You will be able to see PJ's Landing Marina from the navigation channel. To reach the marina, wait until just after you pass this Daymark then turn sharply to starboard toward the entrance to Lackey Creek. Because of shallow water, don't take a shortcut here. As you approach the entrance, water depth will decrease to about 10 feet at normal pool. Beyond the entrance, the creek becomes much wider. Follow the marked channel straight ahead toward the marina. The channel splits and goes around both sides of a small island in front of the fuel dock. Either way, water depth will be about 10 feet at normal pool.

PJ's Landing
2932 Louisville Boat Dock Road
423-984-9001

Open all year, 10AM until 8PM, April 15 to November 1, and 10AM until 5PM the remainder of the year except closed on Monday. Can accommodate boats to 75 feet. Has three transient slips with twin 30 amp electrical service and seven transient slips with some or no electrical service. Water depth at the fuel dock is 10 feet at normal pool. Has gas. Has launch ramp, ice, snacks, showers, and pump out station. Has mechanics on call. Can arrange transportation to nearby grocery. Monitors channel 16. Accepts MasterCard, Visa, Discovery, and American Express credit cards.

MILE 626.9
REPAIR FACILITY

Sinking Creek, the embayment at port, is marked by a sign at the entrance identifying it as the location of the private Fort Loudoun Yacht Club. Past the club's docks and clubhouse and at the end of the embayment is Travis Marine. Be particularly careful about your wake while enroute to this facility.

Travis Marine
9312 Tedford Road
Knoxville, Tennessee 37922
423-690-6700
423-531-2016 (Fax)

This is the only repair facility in the immediate Knoxville area that's directly on the river.

Trailers can haul out boats up to 65 feet. Complete services are available for gas and diesel engines and general repair on all boats except sailboats including props and shafts and painting. There's also a ship store with perhaps the widest selection of boating equipment and supplies on the entire river. Because of limited docking space, call before you bring your boat here. But if you have an emergency and calling first isn't possible, the people at Travis will do all they can to accommodate you.

MILE 630.1

This is the Pellissippi Parkway bridge, Tennessee 162. The Parkway links Oak Ridge and other towns and communities west of Knoxville with Maryville, Alcoa, and the McGhee-Tyson Knoxville Municipal Airport south of the city.

Caution! The wide water ahead is deceptive. As you approach the bridge, be sure to follow the marked channel which hugs the bank at starboard for the next two miles.

MILE 635.2
FUEL

Here, on your port side and just past a cluster of old English style condominiums is the entrance to Duncan Branch. A sign on the upstream side of the entrance indicates Duncan Boat Dock. This is the last place you can refuel enroute to Knoxville.

Enter the marked channel by turning to port just after you pass the green buoy on the main navigation channel. You will see the facility at port soon after you pass between the red and green channel markers. Water depth at the fuel dock is about seven feet at normal pool.

This facility is open 11AM until 7PM, April 1 to November 1. But Ben Duncan, the third member of the Duncan family to operate this dock during the last 50 years, lives in the red house behind the dock. He will pump gas during the off season for anyone who needs it. Also available are snacks, sandwiches, and other supplies. While there, you can also have some fun feeding bread to carp that swim near the dock. For more information, call 423-588-9127.

DAYMARK 641.2

This is the beginning of Sequoyah Hills, one of Knoxville's fine residential areas. Soon, you will be passing Sequoyah Park which borders the river for nearly two miles.

MILE 642.8
ANCHORAGE

This is Looney Island, the last good anchorage before you reach downtown Knoxville. Enter the water on the backside of the island just downstream of the green buoy. Go past the launch ramp where the water is slightly wider. Water depth here will be about 20 feet at normal pool. The amount of current will depend on how much water is being released at Ft. Loudoun Dam. Wind protection is minimal but will be best from the east and the west. The wooded island on one side and Sequoyah Park on the other makes for a pleasant environment. Even if you don't stay overnight, if you have a dinghy, this is a good place to go ashore for a walk in the park.

MILE 643.0

Here, the river skirts busy Alcoa Highway, U.S. 129 and Tennessee 15, which link Maryville, Alcoa, and the McGhee-Tyson Knoxville Municipal Airport with downtown Knoxville.

MILE 643.5

As you come out of the turn you will see part of the University of Tennessee's agricultural research farm at starboard.

Just beyond the next turn are twin spans of the James E. Karnes bridge, U.S. 129.

As you approach the bridge, look to port. The large white house with the terraced gardens extending down the hill to the water is the Armstrong-Lockett house. It was built in 1834 by Drury Paine Armstrong and is one of Knoxville's most historic structures. Inside is the William P. Toms collection of 18th Century English and American furniture, decorative art, and an outstanding collection of English silver. The Italianate style gardens include fountains and extensive plantings.

At port after you pass under the bridge is part of the University of Tennessee campus devoted to agriculture and veterinary science. On the other side on top of the hill is the University's medical center.

Reduce your speed in this area. The bank here is unusually vulnerable to erosion caused by wakes.

MILE 646.6

This is the CSX Railroad bridge.

MILE 647.3

This is the Southern Railroad bridge. As you pass under it, you will see the University of Tennessee's Thompson-Boling Assembly Center & Arena. Although mainly used for basketball games, it also is used for concerts and other special events.

Nearby is Neyland Stadium whose 102,854 seats make it the largest on-campus stadium in the Nation. For the 1996 Tennessee-Florida game, 107,608 spectators crowded into the stadium to set an attendance record unmatched in the history of college football.

The stadium was named after General Robert Neyland. During his remarkable career as head coach, he led the University of Tennessee Volunteers through 9 undefeated seasons out of 21 seasons and to the national championship in 1951. In 1939 during the regular 10-game season, his team held every opponent scoreless while scoring 212 points.

Caution! Because the river is narrow here, your wake can damage boats and docks and raise boat owner tempers to the boiling point. Go slow!

You can now see downtown Knoxville. The tower topped with the gold ball is a reminder that Knoxville is one of the few cities to have hosted a World's Fair. The fair, held in 1982, was attended by more than 11 million visitors.

Knoxville traces its beginning back to 1757 when the British built Fort Loudoun, their first important outpost west of the Allegheny Mountains. In 1786, James White, founder of Knoxville, built a home and stockade on the east edge of the present downtown area. The home still stands.

Other historically important structures include Blount mansion, one of the first wooden frame houses built west of the Appalachian Mountains.

In Knoxville's early days, the river was regarded as an important resource in the city's growth. But its use was so hampered by hazards such as rapids, shoals and whirlpools that many mariners believed Knoxville would remain unreachable by steamboat. In the early 1800s, however, a group of Knoxville businessmen advertised a prize to the first steamboat to come all the way up river to Knoxville. Captain S. D. Conner answered the challenge and began the long trip aboard the "Atlas," a small side wheeler. His effort was successful. On the evening of March 3, 1828, he arrived to collect the reward.

Today, Knoxville is rated as one of the best American cities in which to live. Its population is about 165,000 but county population is nearly twice that. Knoxville is eastern Tennessee's primary cultural, educational, and commercial center.

It also is the gateway to Great Smoky Mountains National Park. The park has more than a half million acres of magnificent scenery, lush foliage, and a wide range of wildlife. It has more visitors than any other national park.

There is much to see and do in and around Knoxville. If you're thinking about staying in the area a few days, your best bet is to leave your boat at a marina and rent a car.

MILE 647.4
DOCKAGE

This is the Henley Street Bridge. On Labor Day the river is crowded with hundreds of boats when this bridge is blocked off and converted into the launching point for a giant fireworks display. Appropriately, the event is called "Boomsday."

You have three options for docking in downtown Knoxville. None of the three docks described have water or electricity, they are available only on a first come first served basis, and you must be willing to accept full responsibility for yourself and your boat. Current and wakes can be bothersome here so double check your lines and fenders to make sure your boat is well secured.

The first option is the dock near the stadium. It's always filled with boats during football weekends.

The second option is a new 450-foot long dock just upstream from the stadium dock. It was built as part of an $8 million riverfront project. Lining the walkway above the dock are fountains and benches and markers that relate interesting facts about Knoxville's history.

The third option is the dock in front of Calhoun's On The River Restaurant which is upstream from the city dock (See mention of this restaurant at Mile 602.6). This dock can accommodate several boats and you can tie up here for as long as you like. You must, however, tell Calhoun's management that you are docked there. For more information, call 423-673-3355.

Even if you don't stay overnight at any of these three docks, docking here for a few hours will allow you to enjoy the heart of Knoxville. Once you walk up the hill past the City County Building and into downtown, you will be only a short distance from Blount Mansion and White's Fort.

The City of Knoxville is planning a new full service marina to be built at First Creek a short distance upstream from the Gay Street Bridge. Nearby will be the Gateway Pavilion, a visitor center which will include retail shops and a restaurant. Although the completion date of this project is uncertain, you can get the latest information by calling the City Architect's Office at 423-215-2040.

MILE 647.7   This is the Gay Street Bridge.

MILE 648.7   This is the South Knoxville Bridge.

MILE 649.0   Beginning at about the same location as the buoys on both sides of the river, the nine-foot navigation channel ends and the seven-foot channel begins. These are, however, guaranteed minimum depths. Actual water depth at normal pool is considerably greater.

Downtown Knoxville quickly disappears and is replaced mostly by farms and woodland.

MILE 650.0

At starboard is Dickinson Island on which is located the Downtown Island Airport. It's used by corporate and private aircraft because of its closeness to downtown Knoxville.

MILE 651.0

At port after you pass the line of channel buoys is the Holston Unit of the University of Tennessee's Agricultural Experiment Station. It's mostly used to produce feed for livestock kept at the University's other research facilities. The large building on top of the hill is Knoxville's Community Service Center.

MILE 652.1

In front of you at port is the mouth of the Holston River. At starboard is the mouth of the French Broad River. Neither can be safely navigated by larger boats for more than a short distance.

A freight train may be rumbling over the bridge that crosses the Holston, workers may be unloading barges tied up at the dock on the far bank of the French Broad, and a few fishermen may be sitting on the bank in between. Yet nothing here suggests that this is the beginning of one of our Nation's greatest rivers.

As you head back downstream and view the scenery from still another perspective, you will appreciate its greatness even more.

What you see may bring you back again and again. As many have discovered, the Tennessee is that kind of river.

A folio of Tennessee River navigation charts prepared by the U.S. Army Corps of Engineers and the Tennessee Valley Authority is updated when needed. The folio contains 118 charts, is spiral bound, and has laminated covers.

The cost of this folio is subject to change. So call or write the Corps at the following address to get the current price. Your check should be made payable to "FAO U.S. Army Engineer Division, Lakes & Rivers Division."

> U. S. Corps of Engineers
> P. O. Box 1070
> Nashville, Tennessee 37202
> 615-736-2950

Here's where you can get tourist information concerning the three states through which the Tennessee River flows:

KENTUCKY

> State Board of Tourism
> 22nd Floor, Capital Plaza Tower
> 500 Mero Street
> Frankfort, Kentucky 40601
> 1-800-225-8747

TENNESSEE

> Department of Tourist Development
> State of Tennessee
> 320 6th Avenue N.
> Nashville, Tennessee 37202
> 615-741-2159

ALABAMA

> Bureau of Tourism & Travel
> State of Alabama
> P. O. Box 4927
> Montgomery, Alabama 36103-4927
> 205-242-4169 or 1-800-252-2262

Here's who to contact for detailed information about towns and counties on or near the Tennessee River. This list is in approximate order from Paducah, Kentucky, upstream to Knoxville, Tennessee.

Paducah-McCracken Covention and Visitors Bureau
P.O. Box 90, 128 Broadway
Paducah, Kentucky 42002-0090
502-443-8783 or 1-800-359-4775

Grand Lakes Chamber of Commerce
P.O. Box 181
Grand Rivers, Kentucky 42045
502-362-4219

Marshall County Tourism Commission
P. O. Box 129
Gilbertsville, Kentucky 42044
502-362-4128 or 1-800-467-7145

Murray-Calloway County Chamber of Commerce
P.O. Box 190
Murray, Kentucky 42071
502-753-5188 or 502-753-5171

Paris-Henry County Chamber of Commerce
P.O. Box 8, 2508 E. Wood Street
Paris, Tennessee 38242
1-800-345-1103

Tennessee's Kentucky Lake Vacation Association
P.O. Box 428
Paris, Tennessee 38242
901-642-5590

Stewart County Chamber of Commerce
P.O. Box 147
Dover, Tennessee 37058
931-232-8290

Northwest Tennessee Tourism
Box 963
Martin, Tennessee 38237
901-587-4213

Benton/Camden Chamber of Commerce
202 West Main Street
Camden, Tennessee 38320
901-584-8395

Hardin County Tourist Board
507 Main Street
Savannah, Tennessee 38372
901-925-2364
1-800-552-3866

Colbert County Tourism & Convention Bureau
P.O. Box 440
Tuscumbia, Alabama 35674
256-383-0783 or 1-800-344-0783
E-mail: shoalstourism@worldnet.att.net

Florence/Lauderdale Tourism
1 Hightower Place
Florence, Alabama 35630
256-740-4141 or 1-888-356-8687

Decatur Convention & Visitors Bureau
P.O. Box 2349, 719 6th Avenue SE
Decatur, Alabama 35602-2349
256-350-2028 or 1-800-524-6181

Alabama Mountain Lakes Tourist Association
P.O. Box 1075
Mooresville, Alabama 35649
256-350-3500 or 1-800-648-5381

Huntsville/Madison County Convention & Visitors Bureau
700 Monroe Street
Huntsville, Alabama 35801
256-551-2230

Marshall County Tourism Commission
P.O. Box 711
Guntersville, Alabama 35976
256-582-7015

Chattanooga Area Convention & Visitors Bureau
2 Broad Street
Chattanooga, Tennessee 37402
423-756-8687 or 1-800-322-3344

Chamber of Commerce
384 Front Street, P.O. Box 355
Spring City, Tennessee 37381
423-365-5210

Chamber of Commerce
107 Main Street
Dayton, Tennessee 37321
423-775-0361

Roane County Tourism Bureau
P.O. Box 1033
Kingston, Tennessee 37763
423-376-4201

Loudon County Visitors Bureau
1075 Highway 321 N.
Lenoir City, Tennessee 37771
423-986-6822

Monroe County Tourism Council
4765 Highway 68
Madisonville, Tennessee 37354
423-442-9147 or 1-800-245-5428

Knoxville Convention & Visitors Bureau
810 Clinch
Knoxville, Tennessee 37902
423-523-7263 or 1-800-727-8045

The Land Between The Lakes Recreational Area (LBL) borders the Tennessee River from Mile 25.3 to Mile 66.2. This peninsula between Lake Barkley and Kentucky Lake offers 170,000 acres of splendid outdoor recreational opportunities and scenic beauty. Also, the LBL has special exhibit areas, a visitor center, and a year around schedule of events. If the staff knows in advance you are coming, they will try to make special arrangements for your visit. Contact:

> The Land Between The Lakes
> 100 Van Morgan Drive
> Golden Pond, Kentucky 42211-9001
> 502-924-2000

Here's a list of state parks that are directly on the Tennessee River:

> Kentucky Dam Village State Resort Park
> P.O. Box 69
> Gilbertsville, Kentucky 42044
> 502-362-4271

> Kenlake State Resort Park
> 542 Kenlake Road
> Hardin, Kentucky 42048
> 502-474-2211

> Paris Landing State Resort Park
> 400 Lodge Road
> Buchanan, Tennessee 38222
> 901-642-4311

> Pickwick Landing State Resort Park
> P.O. Box 15
> Pickwick Dam, Tennessee 38365
> 901-689-3135

> Joe Wheeler State Park
> P.O. Drawer K
> Rogersville, Alabama 35652
> 256-247-5461

> Lake Guntersville State Park
> 1155 Lodge Drive
> Guntersville, Alabama 35976-9126
> 256-582-2061 or 1-800-548-4553

> Harrison Bay State Recreational Park
> Route 2, Box 118
> Harrison, Tennessee 37341
> 423-344-6214

If this book has been helpful, then you may want to know about the other two CruiseGuides written and published by Fred Myers. They are ideal companions for use with the official charts.

The Cumberland River CruiseGuide is your passport to one of America's most undiscovered rivers. Emptying into the Ohio River and paralleling the Tennessee River for more than 60 miles, the Cumberland's 352-mile navigation channel extends eastward to provide boaters access to Nashville, Music City U.S.A. Beyond Nashville, the river offers many scenic treats as it skirts the western edge of the Cumberland Plateau. This is the only cruising guide devoted exclusively to the Cumberland. $18.00 postpaid.

The Tenn-Tom Nitty-Gritty CruiseGuide strips away confusion, misinformation, and rumors to reveal what boaters really want to know about the Tennessee-Tombigbee Waterway. The Tenn-Tom, as it's usually called, is the 450-mile link between the Tennessee River and the Gulf Coast. From northern Mississippi to southern Alabama, you will find the Tenn-Tom to be one of the Nation's most unique stretches of navigatable water. You will want this invaluable book beside you for every mile of it. $19.00 postpaid.

Send your order to: CruiseGuides, 803 Hermitage Drive, Suite 112, Florence, Alabama 35630. If you would like more information from Fred before ordering, call him at 256-766-4802.

Fred is available for lectures and instruction to associations, yacht clubs, educational institutions, and other organizations concerned with recreational interests on the inland river system. To discuss the possibilities, call him at 256-766-4802 or send e-mail to: writerfred@aol.com